The Seed of Civilization

The Origins of War, Marriage, and Religion

by
Norman Pedersen

Published in 2017 by SóL-Earth Publishers
Copyright © 2017 by Norman Pedersen
All rights reserved

Printed in United States of America

ISBN 978-1978169531

The Seed of Civilization
The Origins of War, Marriage, and Religion

Preface   page 5

Introduction   page 7

Part I. Before Civilization

1. Biases With Which We Perceive Prehistory   page 13

2. Analysis of Prehistoric Cave Art   page 21

3. Analysis of Hunter-Gatherer Peoples   page 37

4. Change   page 49

5. The Psychological Shift   page 57

6. Corollaries to the Psychological Shift   page 77

Part II. The Creation of Civilization

7. Ego, the Seed of Civilization   page 85

8. Doubt and Loss   page 91

9. Order From Chaos   page 99

10. Words and Language   page 107

11. Competition   page 115

12. Hierarchies   page 123

13. Supernatural   page 129

14. Conclusion   page 135

Bibliography   page 142

Preface

The prehistoric cave paintings of France have fascinated me since I saw photos of Lascaux in my mother's Paris Match magazines. I could not have been more than eight years old. But even then I was taken in by the romance of subterranean artistic treasures tens of thousands of years old. Some fifty years later I spent time in France visiting sites of prehistoric cave art and culture. It was extraordinary. The reality of these works cannot be grasped in photos. They must be experienced in situ. They are so remarkable and so old that one instinctively begins to wonder at the whole venture of human achievement.

Without prodding or guidance my unrelenting brain donned deerstalker cap, took up tobacco pipe, and pursued these ancient clues. I simply followed the lead and accompanied my Holmesian instincts. Logical deductions were made, and a broad investigation into the people who had created these works was launched. Over the years that investigation spread to the dark recesses of a score of academic disciplines. I recorded the adventure in *When Was the Name of God First Spoken, Correcting Misconceptions about Prehistory*.

It was never my intention to write this book.

Writing *The Seed of Civilization* became a necessity after I wrote *When Was the Name of God First Spoken*. That book had grown and had taken shape of its own accord as I followed an intellectual curiosity. Ultimately, it was a rambling through the author's brain as he became aware of fascinating understandings about human society before 10,000 years ago. The research revealed our forebears to have been quite unlike ourselves. So different, in fact, that our self-image was put into question. But some readers failed to grasp the full import of what the author's research had revealed.

Thus the necessity for *The Seed of Civilization*.

It is to be short and concise. It will decipher a humanity formerly unknown. It will raise questions in the reader's mind. It will stimulate incredulity. But the ideas offered herein are valid and provable. They are facts that should not be taken on faith. They should be held and tasted and ruminated until every nuance is obvious, rational, and undeniable.

Then we must look at ourselves with a completely different mirror.

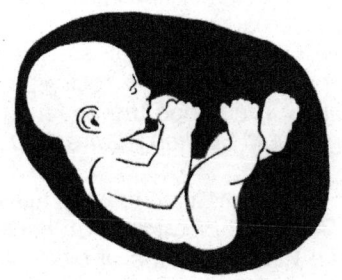

Introduction

Before you begin this book take a minute to look at a newspaper or a news website. Whenever you happen to do that, there is a certainty that military conflict, crime in its many manifestations, and political turmoil locally, nationally, and globally will be prominently displayed. It has always been so. Throughout mankind's history the evidence of human aggression is blatantly conspicuous. The track of history through time is paced by military and political power struggles, by one people attempting to dominate others.

Defining the behavior of our species requires a vocabulary of aggression, domination, coercion, emotional and physical violence, social prejudices, political biases, and irrational fears of the unknown. We assume that this is the inherent nature of mankind, of our homo sapiens species. But these are only the behaviors of Civilized man. For 150,000 years before the coming of Civilization human beings were a different people.

Before you begin this book take another minute to define what characterizes human civilizations. Government, laws and enforcement, social rules and consequences, religious beliefs and rituals, hierarchies of social and political status... all are the trappings of Modern Civilized man. In whatever manner you define Civilization, no aspect of that definition existed in human societies prior to 10,000 years ago.

We have long assumed that even the most primitive societies had certain minimal cultural absolutes. All human societies have had ceremonies for marriage, birth, death, and coming of age. Every group has had a leader, usually a strong, dominant male or a sage elder. All people have had sports and competitive games. Every culture has had religious leaders and rituals to help intercede with the Supernatural. We assumed this of every culture, clan, society, or tribe going back into distant prehistory.

Our assumptions have been completely wrong. We have ignored first-hand evidence and failed to connect that evidence to obvious correlation with our Stone Age ancestors.

Civilization is not the result of tens of thousands of years of continuous human progress. Civilization was birthed some several thousand years before recorded history.

Civilization is a mere 9,000 years old or less. Homo sapiens, modern human beings, have been inhabiting this planet for more than 160,000 years.

The genesis of human Civilization had a seed, a direct and definable cause. People had lived a stable, unchanging lifestyle for 150,000 years before Civilization began.

Then something changed.

It is now possible to authoritatively state when, how, and why that change occurred and human Civilization began.

Philosophers, anthropologists, and biologists; sociologists, linguists, and psychologists have constantly sought an answer to the question that seems to hound mankind. "What separates Man from Beast?" For 150,000 years the answer to that question was, "Nothing." No one even bothered to ask the question. It was meaningless.

For 150,000 years homo sapiens, the same biological human beings as we are today, lived as all other living things that have inhabited this Planet Earth. They were intelligent and social and enjoyed life as do many higher animal species. They followed the biological and evolutionary imperatives of doing what was necessary for an efficient survival of the species. They had no Civilization or even the germ of Civilization. Homo sapiens were simply a very clever species quite adept at observing the natural environment and at making tools to augment their limited physical abilities. Maintaining an optimally small population for 150,000 years the species thrived.

About 10,000 years ago, at the same time as the beginnings of agriculture, human beings unwittingly diverged from the natural way of things, and the world has not been the same since. Civilization sprang to life with cities and governments and religions and social status. History, philosophy, poetry, mathematics, and the sciences were born. The written word sparked an intellectual revolution.

Human beings transformed the very definition of life. What had once been the natural, common everyday of living became chaos, and chaos then required order to tame and rein it in.

Human beings also transformed themselves.

Everything we have thought we knew about the character of human beings is incorrect. We assume that the motives and emotions we exhibit today have been the same for all people throughout time.

We assume the character of man to be aggressive, often violent, and capable of irrational rage. It is an obvious, self-evident truth.
History proves it.
Now prehistory disproves it.
These acknowledged innate characteristics of man are completely opposite to what human beings were. For 150,000 years we were quite a different people. All human beings living before 10,000 years ago were a kinder, gentler people. It might seem impossible to prove this, but there are sufficient clues and enough facts to be convincing.
The question to be answered is, "If human beings were non-aggressive and nonviolent for 150,000 years how and why did they become murderous, vicious, and abusive?" Because that was not a small insignificant change. It was a radical, complete reversal of human behaviors and social order.

The Seed that brought forth Civilization came from within human beings born after the advent of agriculture. It germinated and grew within the human psyche. It fostered a change in human behavior so disruptive that the species was in danger of extinction.
Civilization was evolved from a necessity to survive.
Civilization became the solution and salvation.

This book is divided into two parts.
The first part, entitled Before Civilization, is a straightforward presentation of the evidence revealing the change in human behavior which occurred about 10,000 years ago.
Before presenting that evidence there is a prerequisite look at some of the acquired prejudices each of us carries without awareness. It is a caveat: approach the information and ideas about prehistory with full, open-minded, cerebral acuity.
Clues found in the prehistoric cave art of France and Spain are analyzed. They are the only link with prehistory that can reveal anything about the minds and attitudes of our Ice Age ancestors.
There is a quick survey and assessment of hunter-gatherer societies and the people who lived this lifestyle. Logically, all persons living before human efforts at agriculture (about 10,000 years ago) lived as nomadic hunter-gatherers.
There is an itemizing of the changes that agriculture brought to the hunter-gatherer lifestyle.

Finally, Chapter 5 reveals the dramatic psychological disruption that affected human beings as they turned to agriculture.

The second part of this book, entitled The Creation of Civilization, is an analysis of the mechanisms that worked to fabricate human Civilization.

The ultimate motivation for the creation of Civilization is unveiled and revealed to be the human ego. Egos have generated the myriad aspects of our Modern culture with specific purpose and method. The growth of Civilization was organic.

Psychological doubt was the underlying need for Civilization. Hunter-gatherers never had it. Modern egos have struggled with it and have over-compensated for it continuously.

Chapter 10 explains how language was an integral factor in the creation of Civilization. Civilization would not exist without the abstract symbolism of words. Key points about the phenomenon of verbal abstraction are linked to the development of modern thinking.

The various aspects of Civilization are discussed:

Competition, a seemingly perfectly natural activity, was actually fostered by Civilization.

The role of hierarchal status and social structure as they give order to Modern populations is analyzed.

Magic, Supernatural, and fantasy are shown to be the brain children of Civilization.

In conclusion we will examine the relevance of these findings to a better understanding of our species and ourselves as individuals.

Part I. Before Civilization

1. Biases With Which We Perceive Prehistory

Before we blithely approach the subject of our human ancestors it is necessary to take a look at ourselves and consider what intellectual and psychological baggage we may carry. Even in our most open-minded and insightful moments we are rarely mindful of the biases that short-circuit our mental endeavors. It is especially important to realize that these prejudices have been acquired. They were not inherently a part of human experience.

The following are biases with which we approach prehistory and indeed many academic disciplines. They are so ingrained in our cultural thought that they affect our thinking without our being aware of them. They did not exist in human thinking 100,000 years ago or 50,000 years ago or 20,000 years ago. They were born less than 10,000 years ago at the same time as human Civilization.

Anthropocentrism

Anthropocentrism is simply "man-centered". Man comes first in all considerations. It is not a conscious thing. It is not an ideology. It is an assumption that underlies all human thinking.

Perception, problem-solving, and philosophy are all based on the assumption that human beings are more important than other life forms. Human beings are the focus. Everything else is considered and evaluated in relationship to man. Does it benefit mankind? Is it an impediment to human efficiency? How can it be put to good use, with the understanding that good use is in terms of personal or cultural need or whim?

This self-centered focus ultimately gives way to an understanding that humans are superior to all other life forms. Man is the culmination of evolution. Man is the steward of the earth; man has dominion over all.

Man has language beyond the squawk, chatter, and bark of other animals. His words allow him to communicate the most esoteric of intellectual ideas. He has invented the written word and has produced millions of books to keep statistics, to catalog history, and to communicate philosophy and emotional experience.

Man has created mathematics with which to translate all things, real or imaginary, into numeric symbols. The most profound and the most infinitesimal are itemized.

Man has created a technology of complex tools that enable him to do impossible things. He can move mountains of earth and stop the flow of rivers. He can fly around the globe. He has even been to the moon and back. He can survive any extreme of climate or geography: in underwater depths, in subzero temperatures, in thin atmospheres upon the highest mountains, and in the mouth of molten volcanoes. He can clone life.

Man has manipulated every possible energy: fire, electricity, light, heat, cold; nuclear.

Man has triumphed over every other creature he has chosen to confront or which has chosen to confront him from the fiercest of lions or bears or bulls to the most cunning of bacteria or insect or fungus. He has domesticated many to his needs and wishes.

Yes, it is quite obvious that human beings are superior to all they survey. But it is only evident to human beings. We are certainly a unique species, but only superior from our own viewpoint.

Without anthropocentrism human beings are simply homo sapiens, another of the living organisms populating this planet.

Anthropocentrism may seem like a natural enough thing. But it is a modern understanding. It was not always a part of human thought because there was never a need to be superior to anything.

The Seed of Civilization changed that.

Progress

Progress is the pervasive optimistic thinking that as things grow and increase they get better. Age brings wisdom. Knowledge brings truth. Maturity brings emotional balance. What is true for individuals is also true for culture and Civilization.

Our present understanding of history and prehistory is linear. One thing follows another. Actions beget reactions and stimulate successive events. Political and social events have cause and then effect. Philosophies and academic studies are built on that which came before. We analyze and modify. We amend and append. We keep the good and discard the bad.

With such an understanding it is logical to conclude that things improve as time passes. We expect that every change in human Civilization and technology is an improvement. We only get better and better. We assume that our understandings and thinking are clearer than that of previous generations. We are more rational, less superstitious. We continue to refine theory and technique for dozens of sciences. We have more data and more factual knowledge. We are more socially sensitive. Our communications technologies have improved beyond imagination. Mechanical technologies have not only allowed one man or one soldier to do the work of ten, but in many cases have replaced human workers. Life is easy and less burdensome. We build bigger, better, and faster than any previous generation.

Athletes increase and set new standards of performance beyond what was ever dreamed of. As a culture we are more aware of the needs of those less fortunate and who have been demeaned and devalued in the past. We recognize and expose racial, religious, and sexist bigotries. Economically, the common man has never been more comfortable or prosperous. And the rich have never been richer than they are today.

We as a species are smarter, more capable, and more human than any who have come before. Such is the thinking that pervades any look at history. Yet it is a subtle prejudice that fosters a certain condescension towards other cultures and other people and other times. That prejudice colors our perception of data and must be acknowledged if we are to truly understand prehistory.

People are people
When we are told that prehistoric homo sapiens were physically and mentally the same as we are today, we accept it with a grain of salt. They certainly were not as advanced or intelligent or sophisticated as we are today. Even humans living five hundred years ago were not. Those living in the third world nether regions of our planet are fellow human beings, but they certainly are not up to our educated standards. Yet we understand certain things about them knowing that there are commonalities among all people.

We recognize the same expressions of emotions in others. Smiles, scowls, shrugs, and laughter are universally understood. There is no communication barrier to sorrow or joy or fear.

We recognize common behaviors of kindness, selfishness, friendliness, suspicion, and aggression. We are careful to discern such behaviors in those around us and react accordingly. We know the things that motivate and move people. Compassion, love, greed, power, and sex are strong motivators.
Yes, we can look at ourselves and those in other cultures and see the same human behaviors. Life experience teaches us these things. We recognize similar behaviors in the notables and commoners throughout history. World literatures reveal human natures we can see in ourselves and those around us.
So it is a reasonable way of thinking: regarding the nature of human beings, "People are people". We use the knowledge we have available, and it seems valid and conclusive. It may be that human beings have had this same awareness for more than 160,000 years.
There is one little problem with this understanding. What human beings have perceived as characteristic human behavior for the past 10,000 years is very different from what human beings living before that time perceived as characteristic human behavior.
We will see that there are some emotions and behaviors which we deem universal to our species which did not exist 20,000 or 50,000 or 100,000 years ago.
So the idea that, with regard to human nature, "People are people" becomes a subtle exclusionary bias. When we are confronted with human behaviors that seem extraordinary or anomalous we must not dismiss them. We must not wrack and twist them to conform to what we think we know. We must take them at face value until we can examine them closer.

Assumptions with which this book is written
It would not be reasonable to point out today's academic and popular prejudices without acknowledging a central bias with which the author has pursued research and with which he has written this book.
It is worth noting that there was no hypothetical thesis to support when the author's research into prehistoric cave art and hunter-gatherer societies began. Simple curiosity led the way. The subsequent conclusions merely followed the information that was found and pieced together.
The most significant and doubtlessly controversial prejudice that the author brought to his work is the idea that

human babies come into this world without pre-programming. They possess only a small handful of biological and evolutional directives to survive.

This idea, while seemingly very rational, flies in the face of too many personal beliefs, ideologies, fantasies, and scientific hypotheses. The reaction by the vast majority of educated and/or uneducated is to immediately discredit the idea. Genetics is being used as a scientific basis for social behaviors and psychological tendencies, but it is being used merely as a quick explanation for things scientists and sociologists do not fully understand. Without any reason for doing so, philosophers and religious teachers claim that babies come into this world with past lives or innate moral and ethical understanding. Some linguists insist that babies are hard-wired for language grammar structure. None of these things has strong scientific or experiential support. They are opportune explanations and quick theories.

A newborn develops physically from a soft bundle of flesh and blood. It reacts to light and sound and touch, but its eyes are shut. It will reflexively clench something that touches it, and it will suckle when given the opportunity. It is helpless. It would not survive without care and nourishment. It is completely new to the world. It is empty of any thought or intellectual perception.

Locke's *tabula rasa* is not quite the appropriate metaphor. It implies that knowledge is written onto an infant's empty mind. Today we have a better metaphor with the modern electronic computer. Hardware and software. The hardware of the human brain is impressive beyond our comprehension. And what of the software? How complicated an operating system is each of us given? Why not choose the simplest as being most efficient?

A software that processes raw data by searching for patterns seems to suffice. We perceive patterns in the physical world and in human behavior. We see patterns in action and reaction. We associate patterns of human expression, situation, and emotion.

Recognizing patterns is necessary and sufficient to initiate interaction with the physical world. Noting patterns is followed by trial and error imitation of actions and expressions. Trial and error teaches the individual whether the observed pattern is valid. Observe a pattern, then imitate. Obtain feedback and repeat. Verify. That is how physical skills, strategies of action, and interpersonal relations are learned.

Considered rationally, a cerebral operating system that defines patterns is sufficient to acquire technologies, language, and social behaviors. Watching any infant will make it clear that we learn by observation and not by any preprogramming. In these modern times very young girls incredibly develop a sense of fashion. Young boys know every step required to start and drive a car. And all two-year olds know how to interface with a smart phone. None of these were acquired by verbal instruction and certainly not genetically.

Corollary to this bias is the author's specific prejudice against one of the foundations of Freudian psychology. Freud defined sex as a relevant primary motivation in everyone's very early childhood. Libido, castration anxiety, penis envy, and the Oedipus complex are all parts of Freudian childhood development. The pleasure principle guides early (and lifelong) choices and decision making.

I would rather base a child's development on biological and evolutional motivations. From its birth a child grows physically, mentally, emotionally, and psychologically with the sole motivation of doing that which enables it to survive as a living thing. There are too many instances of personal choices that are contrary to choosing pleasure over pain. These examples are easily explained when the motivation is survival rather than gratification.

It is, perhaps, a small thing, a difference of semantics. But it takes psychology away from the lascivious and toward science.

Not 100%

The observations and resultant deductions in this book are not about the 100 percentile.

They are based on the 99% majority of facts. There will be 1% of specific examples that will go against information and conclusions presented.

Finding anomalies does not disprove the observations about the 99% preponderance. Surprisingly, the 1% of anomalies will often reveal the importance of what is expressed by the 99%. They are a useful tool.

Biases

Because of the academic and cultural biases that have attached themselves to our every thought and perception some of the statements in this book will seem unacceptable. Reflexively they will be dismissed. They will be emphatically denied without rationale for doing so.

Biases, once defined, can be recognized and overcome if one should care to do so. It is one of the miracles of language. Once a word is attached to something, once a verbal symbol has been linked to something, the mind can deal with it. It can dissect it, reconstruct it, or completely dismiss it. It can overcome irrational reasoning, deep-rooted fears, conditioned emotional responses, and years of brainwashing.

If something in the following discussion should perturb you, the reader, please pause. Consider the facts without any of the author's conclusions. Eventually the facts will connect and elucidate. A little consideration will show the validity of the information given herein.

Mammoths at Rouffignac

2. Analysis of Prehistoric Cave Art

The story of mankind is at least 150,000 years old. The actual history of mankind, however, is perhaps 6,000 years old. Which simply means that 96% of our ancestry is hidden in the shadows of prehistory. Our knowledge of history is comparatively infinite. Ever since written language was developed men have been eager to write. They have kept evidence of every nuance of human action, mindset, and hidden emotion. We know dates and hours, facts and figures, motivations and methods. Politics, money, military, and divine intercession have been meticulously recorded and interpreted. History has been and continues to be written and rewritten with on-going, in-depth analysis and commentary. Our knowledge of history grows by the minute.

In contrast, our knowledge of prehistory has no verbal record and little physical evidence upon which to reconstruct. We have fossilized skeletons dating back 150,000 to 200,000 years. The anatomical structure revealed by these bones is different enough from previous hominid forms to make us a unique species, homo sapiens. We have some stone tools and bone artifacts that indicate something of the technological capabilities and of the economic lifestyle. Over the millennia there were progressive advances in technology. There are sewing needles and atlatl spear-throwers. There are decorated tools, carved artifacts, and statuettes. It is little from which to understand 150,000 years of human existence.

Fortunately, our Ice Age ancestors left us another kind of physical evidence preserved for tens of thousands of years in subterranean vaults. Dating as far back as 40,000 years ago human beings in Europe painted animal portraits that still exist on cave walls today. They are the only real evidence we have of how Paleolithic humans perceived their world. Surprisingly, this art ceased to be created after the Last Ice Age receded and humans began efforts at agriculture and animal husbandry. The coincidence is not without significance.

The Ice Age cave paintings of southwestern Europe are an astonishing heritage. They are thousands of works created over a span of at least 20,000 years. There is a consistency of technique, style, and subject matter for those twenty millennia.

At Cueva de Altamira in northern Spain there are more than a dozen bison painted on the ceiling of a large underground chamber. Many of them are in unusual positions, curled round upon themselves as if sleeping. The rock ceiling has pronounced undulations, and the bison have been ingeniously shaped to fit the contours of these stony projections. Even in their unique positions the bison are anatomically proportioned with details of horns, eyes, tails, and cloven hooves. The bulging roundness of the ceiling projections upon which the bison are painted in black outline and red accent gives each figure a bulk and mass that adds to the realistic portrayal.

Bison at Altamira

At La Grotte de Rouffignac in France the Frieze of Ten Mammoths has six mammoths standing in one direction and four mammoths facing opposite towards them in an aesthetically pleasing composition. All of the mammoths are quietly imposing. They are shown in side view with some positioned behind others giving perspective depth to the image. They are realistically portrayed, anatomically correct with huge round tusks, and show no emotion. The Frieze of Five Mammoths shows two mammoths facing two mammoths with a smaller mammoth painted in the foreground. All stand level on a line created by irregular rock strata on the wall. The subjects are rendered realistically and without emotion or narrative to the composition, as if four adults and one child had stood quietly to have their portraits done. The Great

Ceiling at Rouffignac has more than forty animals outlined in black paint. There are horses, mammoths, rhinos, bison, and ibex. Many are only partial sketches. They overlap and are scattered in every direction. They range from a life-size horse to a horse's head only several inches big. In all the seeming chaos the ceiling is still a magnificent compilation of artistic endeavor.

At La Grotte de Chauvet walls are covered with hundreds of charcoal sketches. Stylistically many could have been the work of one artist. There are groupings that resemble artists' studies: the head of a horse repeated several times in close proximity; ten lions' heads all in profile in the same direction; rhinoceroses repeated into the distance; bison. The drawings often overlap. A bison's body drawn in profile continues around the curve of wall to a frontal view of its head. And while each of the animals shows character, there is no display of emotion or animation.

At La Grotte de Lascaux there are close to one thousand animals painted, most of which are bulls, horses, bison, and deer. The Hall of Bulls is dominated by six huge bulls, the largest of which is about eighteen feet long. There are seven smaller horses painted alongside, and there are several tiny deer scattered here and there. There is composition and design to the whole room. The paintings are high on the wall, curving onto the ceiling. Most of the animals seem to be heading toward an opening which leads down into the next subterranean chamber. Some animals are placed in harmonious counterpoint facing the opposite direction. All of the images are realistic and in profile view. There are two sets of paintings of horses which can easily be interpreted as sequential art. In the Hall of Bulls five small black horses are painted in a row. The first has its front legs in a low standing position. In the next painting the horse's legs are lifted, bent at the knee. The painting of the third horse has been damaged, and there are no front legs to be seen. In the fourth painting, the horse's legs are lifted and the knees almost straight. In the last image the horse's two front legs are high and fully outstretched in front. The other example of possible animation is a sequence of three horses. The first is standing on the edge of a small projection of stone high on the left wall as one descends into the next chamber. Halfway down on the same side is a horse with its mane blown back. At the bottom of the shaft is a third horse flat on its back with its legs sticking up in the air.

At La Grotte de Font de Gaume there are hundreds of animal paintings. They are primarily bison, horses, deer, and mammoths. The cave is small and narrow. Paintings are often in places hardly accessible and difficult to see. Most of the animals are single portraits, but there are compositional groupings. The subjects are painted in black outline and often infilled with red, brown, or black. The animals are realistically rendered with the surface of the parietal wall giving accent to anatomical features and bodily mass. They are shown fully complete, in profile, standing inanimate.

Nearby there is another cave, La Grotte des Combarelles with more than 400 portraits of bison, horses, bulls, and deer. All were etched into the stone surface. None were painted. The artworks are difficult to see without specifically and carefully directed lighting. This fact wakens the modern tourist to the realization that all prehistoric cave art was created by lamplight in an otherwise pitch black environment.

Inspiration for the Paintings
Cave walls are not smooth flat surfaces. They are subterranean stone and earth aggregations subjected to hundreds of thousands of years of geological compression and erosion. When an artist went into a cave with his handheld tallow lamp the walls became animated by moving shadows. It was in these shadows that prehistoric artists discovered their subjects.

In La Grotte des Combarelles there is an etched horse's head. The artist scratched lines to connect natural features of the rock. The horse's lower neck is a comparatively deep crevice in the rock. The horse's chin, lip, back ear, a small section of muzzle, and cheek are all slight ridges in the natural texture of the wall. The eye has a small round dimple. Given proper lighting each of these seven slight textural features is an accented black shadow. The artist merely completed what he saw suggested in these shadows. His faintly etched lines were also accented by shadows, and the work was much more dramatic than we can see in most photos or by visiting the site in modern lighting.

At La Grotte de Font de Gaume there is a painting of a bison outlined in black and filled in with a dark reddish brown. The profile of the bison's head is a rough ridge of the rocky parietal wall. Its eye is a hole in the surface. The back of the head is indicated by a slight ridge. The bison's characteristic wooly shoulder is a roughly textured plane of the parietal surface. The massive back of the bison is a curving bulge in the wall. Under the animal's tail there is a short, deep natural crevice that coincides with the rump. Another natural crevice is at the juncture of the animal's rear leg and its underbelly. The massive front leg is defined by three features: a deep vertical crevice separating the two front legs, a ridge at the upper leg, and several stony features at the fore where the leg meets the chest. [1.]

Bison at Font de Gaume

It has often been mentioned that prehistoric cave artists incorporated natural features of the parietal surface to accent and augment their works. These comments make the assumption that the artist wanted to paint a specific subject and found a wonderfully suitable place in which to do that. There is a flaw in this thinking which is inherent to Civilized men. It should be quite evident that the artist only decided what to paint after he had seen it indicated in the shadows on the wall. One could search for a lifetime to find a place where ten features of the wall matched the desired image of a bison as at Font de Gaume.

Almost every work of prehistoric art can be found to have at least one natural feature of the parietal wall that was the artist's initial inspiration. The tiny deer wandering through the Hall of Bulls at Lascaux were inspired by ridges of mineral deposits that were painted as the deer's antlers. The heads of five swimming deer were painted at Lascaux above dramatic horizontal strata of rock that took on the aspect of swiftly flowing river waters. The famous spotted horses of Pech-Merle were inspired by the rocky outcropping which is all too obviously the profile of a horse's head. A most unusual painting at Font de Gaume shows one deer licking another prone deer. The tongue is a feature of the stone wall. As already mentioned, the curled bison at Altamira were fitted perfectly to the contour of the rocky projections upon which each was painted. Eyes, mouths, and/or chins of some coincide with crevices, dimples, or stony bulges. The pride of ten lions at Chauvet was inspired by the holes or small round bulges that became their eyes.

If, as would seem to be the case, artists were inspired by what they saw in the shadows of cave walls what can we say about their motivations for creating these works of art? Perhaps it is best not to assign supernatural or drug-induced or paranormal motivations. Perhaps it is best not to try to answer this question until more has been revealed.

Description
A comprehensive overview of the prehistoric cave paintings of France and Spain is essential to understanding the phenomenon of this art.

A generous estimate for the number of paintings is perhaps in the neighborhood of 5,000 animals rendered. The works were created at least as early as 33,000 years ago at Altamira and at Chauvet. There are works that date as late as 13,000 years ago at Font de Gaume and at Rouffignac. Mathematically, that is an average of one small animal painting every four years. But there was not a continuous, slow paced output of work. Nor was there an Art Movement or Explosion of Creativity. The Ice Age paintings were created during scattered epochs. During the span of 20,000 years there were lapses of many thousands of years when no paintings were created. The time scale is huge.

It is obvious that many works were created over short periods of time by individuals intent on their work. The Great Ceiling at Rouffignac has more than forty animals, each considered a separate work. They were most likely done by a single artist, and could have been completed in a matter of days or weeks. Tableaux were seemingly done by one artist who composed the arrangement. The Frieze of Ten Mammoths and the Frieze of Five Mammoths at Rouffignac are good examples. At Chauvet the arrangement of ten lions and the study of four horses are other examples. So the number of artists who created the entire oeuvre of Ice Age cave art need not have been large. There may have been

merely a few dozen skilled painters, some of whom were artistic geniuses.
   There are stylistic similarities that can be found in caves separated by great distances. (A horse at Pech-Merle is stylistically similar to horses painted at Lascaux some 50 miles away.)
   Although there are many scores of caves with paintings or etchings, most contain only a few works. There are perhaps ten major sites with 100 or more images. [Altamira (100+), Chauvet (200+), Lascaux (900), Rouffignac (200+), Font de Gaume (400+), Les Combarelles (400+), Cosquer (175), Trois Frères (350)]
   Painting was not an occupation that set artists apart as some anthropologists seem to suggest when discussing specialization of labor. It contributed nothing to the survival of the small group of hunter-gatherers of which the artist was a member. Painting was an avocation. It was most likely done during the winter months of encampment when food was nearby and life was unhurried.
   Cave exploration was never without forethought. The first requirement for any cave art was to have enough lighting in the form of small tallow lamps. Excavated examples have been studied, and each handheld lamp would have sufficed for about an hour of illumination. Although etched works could be created on the spur of the moment with any available hard, sharp blade, painting required additional preparation. Pigments, brushes, and water for the pigments was needed. Scaffolding was required for some paintings, and this required wood to be brought into the site.
   In most cases the works of art were seemingly not intended for an audience. Although Lascaux, Altamira, and Rouffignac are large caves, many artwork locations are small, narrow, not easily accessible spaces. Paintings were often placed in awkward niches, at great heights, or at great distance from the cave entries. There is no evidence of visits by large groups to the sites of displayed art.

   Stylistically there is a uniformity to the twenty millennia of prehistoric art. All animals were rendered in a realistic style. There is no question as to what animal is being portrayed. There is attention to anatomical details. There is attention to proportion and mass. All but one or two exceptions are side, profile views of the subject. Most animals are shown in fixed poses as if waiting for the artist to complete their portraits. The artists did not attempt to show dramatic action or emotion in their subjects, although they had the skill to do so. Even predators are shown without bared teeth or threat. There is no story-telling in scenes or tableaux. When animals are painted in groups they are placed in aesthetic compositions rather than in aggressive relation to each other. There are many studies of heads and of partial animals. There are often over-lapping outlined subjects. This was probably not a compositional choice, but rather two individual works that happened to be located in the same place. This is easily explained if we consider that works originated from shadowed features on the cave walls.

Regarding artistic technique, these prehistoric works are quite sophisticated. Line rendering with paint was the standard. Often black-outlined subjects would be filled with color. Red, brown, and yellow could be obtained with mineral and ochre pigments. Charcoal was also a popular medium. Etching could be done with stone on stone or simply by running fingers through soft mud-covered wall surfaces as at Rouffignac.

Artists primarily applied paint with brushes. They also used daubing techniques for dotted infills and renderings. They used spraying techniques with pigment blown through hollow-tubes or with pigment sprayed from the mouth. With spraying techniques they would mask areas as do air-brush artists today.

Ice Age artists developed techniques for indicating perspective depth that are still used today. The most common is a partially outlined animal interrupted by the drawing of another animal to indicate that one is in front of another. There is the technique of repeating the back and head profile lines above a fully rendered animal to indicate a row of animals behind the first. Chauvet has a drawing of four rhinoceroses standing one behind another behind another and behind another using this technique. Another technique used to show fore-to-back perspective is the purposeful disconnecting of legs not in the fore. This leaves a gap between the black lines of the leg and the body. This gap technique is a standard in modern ink drawings and cartoon art.

Another standard technique was to show the horns or antlers of an animal in 3/4 view. Animals were shown in full profile view which captures the most recognizable character of quadrupeds. But horns and antlers drawn in strict profile will look as one not two horns or antlers, the fore hiding the

back. So artists twisted the horns and antlers to a 3/4 view which shows both distinctly. This technique continues to be used by cartoonists and was a standard for Cubism and Picasso.
Prehistoric artists did not use shading. Used to indicate mass, shading was often unnecessary on parietal walls accented by shadows.

What did Ice Age artists paint on the cave walls? They painted the common and remarkable fauna that lived with them on the cold, dry land. Mammoths, bison, horses, bulls (aurochs), deer, reindeer, ibex, rhinoceroses, lions, and bears were the principle subjects. Other rarely depicted animals included goats, donkeys, foxes, and fish. Most of the animals were herbaceous. There was no special attention paid to animals typically hunted or to predatory animals. No one species was given exceptional consideration or preference over others. Each subject received the same careful artistic treatment. All were rendered realistically without exaggeration or alteration.

There is no depicted violence.
There are no scenes of animals fighting one another.
There are no hunting scenes.
There are no hunters or quarry being chased.
There are no images of killed animals.
There was no attention to landscapes, sun, or moon.
Occasionally, there is a human form etched or painted.

Analysis

The study of prehistoric cave art may seem like a pleasant but insignificant pastime. However, the true value of such research becomes evident when one compares it to all art that has been created since. It is distinctly different from all art that came after. In fact, it is unique among human graphic expressions.

Most startling is the question of subject matter, the things artists chose to paint. For the last 9,000 years the complete focus of art has been on human beings. There are paintings of men hunting, men in battle, men and women walking, men and women working, and men and women dancing. There are portraits of kings, generals, royal families, beautiful women, farmers, and slaves. It would seem that everything about people is interesting, exciting, and important. Modern art since the Ice Age cave paintings, the art of Civilized man, has had a 99% preoccupation with humanity.

That is a complete reversal of artistic trends, from one extreme to the opposite extreme, without any noticeable transition.

Statistically, less than 1% of prehistoric cave art depicts anything that can possibly be called human. In fact those images which have been labelled as anthropomorphic are rendered completely different from the typical realism used to paint animals.

At Lascaux there are about 900 images of animals. There is one image of a man. The man is lying in front of a bison. His torso is an elongated rectangle with an erect phallus. His legs are straight sticks with right-angled feet. His four-fingered (not five) hands are at the end of two thin lines splayed outward from the neck. There are no elbows or knees. The head of this man resembles the head of a bird more than anything. It is round, hairless, and has a long pointed beak.

Two "human" figures at La Grotte de Trois Frères are said to be shamans in animal costumes because the images are truthfully only half-human. Viewed from the side an antlered figure has the torso, tail, and shoulders of a cervid or equine animal. The raised front legs are half animal, half human, which is to say that they are neither one nor the other. The rear legs are thick and have human knees and toes. The face is otherworldly. It is looking full-front. Two animal ears stick up. Two asymmetrical round eyes stare at the viewer. There is no nose or mouth, but there may be a long beard within the outline of the animal neck. Another etched half-human figure, viewed from the side, is of a bison standing vertically on human rear legs. The tail, torso, head, and front legs are all bison. There is no indication other then the two human legs which are shown from the knees down that the figure is not a real bison.

The etched human figure at La Grotte de St. Cirq is viewed from the side. It is unclothed and bald. On the round head, turned to 3/4 profile, there are indications of ear, nose, mouth and eye. Thin, bent arms and legs taper to an absence of hands and feet. The torso is round and full-bellied. Hairless and soft, the image could easily represent a newborn infant.

There are more than 400 etchings of animals at Les Combarelles. There are also three etchings which are described as female human torsos. They have no feet, no arms, no hands, and no heads. Truthfully, they could just as well be curved lines in close proximity to one another. For argument's sake we will accept the estimation that the awkwardly incised lines represent women's bodies. If they are female torsos and thighs, they are viewed from the side and have no anatomical correctness. What they do possess are vague suggestions of feminine curves.

Feminine forms at Combarelles

The point to be made about the human depictions found in prehistoric caves is that on the rare occasions when artists did attempt to create human figures the resultant work was less than believable. It is obvious from the thousands of remarkable animal images that prehistoric artists possessed sufficient skill to realistically render whatever animals they chose to portray. But all of the works believed to be of human beings lack such artistic conviction. Why should this be so?

Change
The shift of focus in subject matter is only one of several dramatic changes to artistic trends that occurred after the receding of the Last Ice Age 11,000 years ago. There are intact murals found in the excavated ruins of Çatal Huyuk that clearly bring these changes to light.

The site at Çatal Huyuk is in the Anatolia region of present-day Turkey. It was an ancient city from 9,400 to 8,000 years ago with a population that varied from 3,000 to 8,000 persons. On smooth, almost-white plastered walls were found numerous polychrome paintings. The murals showed humans and animals in highly dynamic poses. The paintings have an abstract, less than realistic, and narrative style. The human figures in the paintings are rubbery-limbed stick-figures. Their heads are round blobs, their feet are mere right-angle stubs at the bottoms of their legs, and their hands are nonexistent. Some figures sport semi-attached leopard skins at their waists and/or their heads. One scene shows dozens of men painted in red or black surrounding a disproportionately large red bovine creature. The creature stands from hoof to withers at least four times the height of any of the men. The bovine head is in profile. Its horns are drawn twisted full-front. It has no eyes. It has no neck. The men are placed in two dimensions all around the animal, at front, sides, under, and over. There is no spatial reality. But there is a lot of animation! Men are running with arms raised up, carrying bows or sticks. Every elbow is bent. The leopard skin attire of those so clothed is flared and splayed from the body. The bovid has its tongue sticking from its mouth; its tail is lifted. Its legs are stiff and straight down to its cloven hooves. Other tableaux show deer with heads in profile and antlers drawn twisted in full-front view. They have no eyes. They are surrounded by disproportionately smaller human figures gesticulating frantically. Other illustrated animal figures can only be described as quadrupeds, having no other distinguishing features. Truthfully, the animals look dead with their tongues hanging from their mouths and their legs extended straight from the bodies at angles that certainly would not support the weights of the torsos. Men are always in full action, and there are lots of men, hunting and triumphing over unrealistically much larger quarry.

Çatal Huyuk mural

What is obvious when comparing prehistoric cave paintings to the paintings found at Çatal Huyuk is that realism was forsaken for representational rendering, that portraiture was replaced by narrative story-telling, and that quiet static figures transitioned to emotion-filled, animate characters.

The paintings at Çatal Huyuk are merely the oldest known works that reflect the change in artistic styles from paleolithic prehistoric to Modern Civilized. Prehistoric cave artists portrayed the animals they observed in the world around them as accurately and realistically as possible. Proportion and anatomical detail were conveyed because they were the simple, natural reality of what was observed. The prehistoric cave artists painted and etched with their eyes. Later artists painted with their minds.

There are examples to be found all around the globe of art created after the Last Ice Age ended and human beings were given a warmer, more fertile world in which to live. This art is always about people. This art never attempts realism. It is not portraiture. It is cerebrally inspired. It intends to communicate, to express, to tell you something. Humans are representational, symbolically abstract. Navaho, Australian aboriginal, and African arts show no regard for anatomical correctness when rendering the human figure. Even as civilizations, such as the Assyrian, Egyptian, and Mayan civilizations, became more sophisticated and the human figure looked more life-like it remained abstractly representational, with stiff limbs and intellectually idealized proportions. Status was indicated in the relative sizes of the figures. There was no attempt or concern for realistic perspective. There was less concern for aesthetic composition than for narrative meaning.

Art for the past 10,000 years has told stories and recorded events. It has told of hunting chases, of victories on the battlefield, of religious visions, and of day-to-day life. Paintings have recorded coronations, news-worthy disasters, wartime surrender, and eternal damnation. Art has sought to communicate something that the artist wanted to relate. It has had intellectual purpose and motivation. What has become important is the message. That cannot be said for 99% of prehistoric cave art. Ice Age art was non-narrative.

By comparison with all art that came afterwards, the oeuvre of prehistoric cave art is sedate, poised, and static. More recent art is filled with action and aggression. Neither people nor animals stand still. Everything runs and jumps, humans chase, hurl weapons, and cheer with wide-spread arms and legs. There is violence. Animals are aggressive, attacking each other and lesser animals. Men are more aggressive, chasing and killing game and confronting and killing other men. Even in death animals are expressive with abnormally stiff legs, closed eyes, extended tails, and straight tongues protruding from their mouths.

99% black to 99% white

For 20,000 years prehistoric cave paintings were the very definition of art. Something changed, and they became an anomaly, the antithesis of all art since. Ninety-nine percent became one percent, and one percent suddenly became the ninety-nine percent normal. It would seem that there is some significance in that shift.

If 99% of art for the past 10,000 years has been focused on human beings, we can say that there has been an anthropocentric bias exhibited by artists and culture for those years. We can say this only because we have noticed that prehistoric cave art did not have such a bias, that only 1% of its works had even an inkling of human anatomy.

In fact, it would seem that Ice Age art was indifferent to men. There is no anthropocentric bias evident in Ice Age prehistoric cave art. Paleolithic cave artists painted and etched what they saw revealed in the shadows of lamplight. What did their imaginations behold in those shadows? It was not human beings. They saw the large, dramatic fauna that were imposing in their everyday world.

The imaginations of Modern Civilized artists and of Modern Civilized men and women have a different focus. Their imaginations think about human beings, and Modern, Civilized art is stimulated from their imaginations.

The lack of anthropocentrism

In summation of the above analysis it should be quite clear that human artistic endeavor underwent a cataclysmic shift. It was not a slow transitioning of styles. Everything changed quickly and radically. What had been the norm for more than 20,000 years disappeared.

We have analyzed the prehistoric cave art of southwestern Europe and compared it to all other human graphic art since. In doing so we have discovered that there is strong evidence that Ice Age artists did not possess an anthropocentric bias. Civilization has long accepted that an anthropocentric bias was natural and innate. Now there is a twinge of doubt about such an assumption.

This, in and of itself, is interesting but cannot be said to be more than that. However, when we can relate it to something that academic scholars have known for 100 years but failed to recognize as significant to the study of prehistory, it is earth-shattering.

    Anthropologists have known that prehistoric groups were nomadic hunter-gatherers. They have known that nomadic hunter-gatherer societies living in the 19th and 20th centuries seemd to be societal anaomalies. They lacked some of the presumed essentials necessary for any human society. They had no leaders. They lived without social hierarchies or status. They were non-aggressive and non-confrontational. In many ways they were unlike all other societies and all other people in the Civilized world today.

    Noticeably the world view of nomadic hunter-gatherers was devoid of an anthropocentric bias.

Chapter notes

1. Norman Pedersen, YouTube website: Prehistoric Art: How to Paint Cro-Magnon, https://www.youtube.com/watch?v=OVx1N7aPsaY

3. Analysis of Hunter-Gatherer Peoples

In the introduction of this book it was stated that people living 20,000 years ago had none of the trappings of Civilization. They had no rulers or laws or social hierarchies. They had no religious ritual, no marriages, and no burial ceremonies. How do we know this? Certainly not by assumptions based on analysis of prehistoric cave art.

Before 10,000 years ago all human beings had a lifestyle defined by anthropologists as hunter-gatherer subsistence. To use the term lifestyle seems to imply a choice, but there was no choice. Before agriculture all human beings hunted and foraged for food.

So for 150,000 years all of humanity lived as hunter-gatherers. Let us begin with that.

Anthropologists have designated simple and complex hunter-gatherer societies, the difference being that simple hunter-gatherers are nomadic or semi-nomadic, and complex hunter-gatherer societies live in fixed domiciles and store food for extended periods of time. This would seem a bit of academic nit-picking except for the fact that the personalities and the social behaviors of the two groups are vastly different.

Simple hunter-gatherer societies are unlike any other groups of human beings. They are certainly without any of the accoutrements of Civilization. They have no leaders or political hierarchies. They are socially egalitarian; everyone is equal in status. These two facts alone separate them from complex hunter-gatherer societies and from all other Civilized societies.

Why should this be?

Even though anthropologists have established these descriptive categorizations they have not given legitimate reasons for why the dramatic differences exist. There seem to be too many contradictions, too many examples to disprove possible theories. They describe complex hunter-gatherer societies as having greater populations and increased possessions with a possible link between these facts and the changes in social dynamics.

Anthropologists struggle with the idea of warfare and whether or not it existed among hunter-gatherers. Studies have confirmed both that it did exist and that there was no warfare among hunter-gatherers. How can either be proved?

All of the theories about hunter-gatherer lifestyles have been conjecture without sufficient information or rationale to make definitive conclusions. There is not enough valid raw data. Studies on indigenous peoples are always contaminated by association with Civilized societies. Asking questions or positioning an outsider as scientific observer immediately skews any collected information.

It would seem an unsolvable dilemma.

However, we may be able to use the very broad and basic information that anthropologists have established to build a viable, all-inclusive, rational explanation.

For 150,000 years all of humanity lived as hunter-gatherers. Consideration of global climatic factors during the Last Ice Age would seem to necessitate at least a semi-nomadic lifestyle. There is evidence to show that people lived in small groups of about 35 people or less. There is no evidence to show that people lived in permanent housing more than 11,000 years ago. These facts help us conclude that human beings living before the receding of the Last Ice Age lived as simple hunter-gatherers, not complex hunter-gatherers.

Let us look at simple hunter-gatherer societies. We must admit that educated people, Civilized people, have acquired cultural biases that influence what they see and how they think. It has been very difficult to get a clear, untainted understanding of the hunter-gatherer societies they have met. But anthropologists can agree on some things.

Simple hunter-gatherers lived nomadic or semi-nomadic lifestyles with stone-age technologies. They hunted for meat and foraged for whatever root vegetables, grains, or seasonal fruits, berries, nuts, and vegetables were available. They maintained a sustainable relationship with the environment and did not over-harvest plants or animals. They used fire and cooked their food. They made their own tools. Their possessions were minimal.

Simple hunter-gatherers had no leaders. No one told others what to do or how to do it or when to do it. No one represented the group. Socially, all members of the group were equal in status. There were no social hierarchies, no patriarchies or matriarchies. Men and women had equal say. Neither youth nor age held higher esteem. Simple hunter-

gatherers shared food with the whole group. This was an absolute.
These are the things anthropologists will agree on. There is much more to be said about simple hunter-gatherers, but scholars hold to their individual opinions. Simple hunter-gatherers were fragile when confronted by Civilization. They were guileless, non-aggressive, and friendly. Civilized men were not. Civilized men came with intent to conquer, to colonize, or to convert. They came with steel knives, with guns, with attitudes of superiority, and with alcohol. They had laws. They had religion. They had possessions. Simple hunter-gatherers had none of these. They were willing to accept some of these things, but such gifts were not harmless. Hunter-gatherer societies could collapse overnight when confronted by the ways of Civilization. So reports and characterizations of simple hunter-gatherer societies have been questionable at best. Because we have looked at them from our world and assumed that they were a part of that world. They have never been a part of our world. Their world is that which existed for 150,000 years before the Seed of Civilization changed it.

Given the intellectual predicament of determining the exact nature of simple hunter-gatherers we are not without hope. We simply need to find somewhat unbiased accounts of isolated indigenous peoples mostly untouched by Civilization.
The Australian aboriginals would seem a good source to study. They remained relatively isolated for perhaps 70,000 years until the 18th century. Unfortunately, there was little desire to study the lifestyle of these indigenous peoples before Europeans colonized the continent and placed it under Civilized rule. Th few studies seem severly biased.
In Africa some tribes living primarily as hunter-gatherers have been documented. The Hadza people of Tanzania and the Mbuti pygmies of the Ituri rainforest in the Democratic Republic of the Congo have been hunter-gatherers living in small groups and having no leaders. They were described as characteristically non-aggressive. Their societies lend support to generalizations about simple hunter-gatherers. Although they remain simple hunter-gatherers these groups have been influenced in some ways by proximity to neighboring peoples. They have also been perceived with obvious cultural biases by outsiders.
We will focus on two other well-documented groups.

Polar Eskimos and Kalahari Ju/wasi
　　Greenland Eskimos remained isolated from Europeans into the late 19th century. Anthropologists took interest in these Eskimo peoples and many scholarly writings described their simple hunter-gatherer societies. Peter Freuchen was a Danish trader who married a Greenland Eskimo woman and lived among those Polar Eskimos from 1905 until 1915. He wrote anecdotal accounts of his life there and of his observations of the culture.
　　In the Kalahari Desert of southern Africa an indigenous people lived isolated from Civilization until 1950 when they were visited by the Marshall family from the United States. The four Americans went with the specific purpose of finding and studying these Ju/wasi (also known as !Kung, San, and San bushmen). Both Lorna Marshall and her daughter, Elizabeth Marshall Thomas, wrote books about their experiences. Following the Marshall's initial research anthropologists studied the Ju/wasi for more than two decades.
　　The sources just mentioned provide a startling insight into simple hunter-gatherer societies living in opposite extremes of climate. The similarities are quite convincing and should be sufficient to define generalizations regarding simple hunter-gatherer societies and the individuals living within those societies.

Economic structure
　　Both the Ju/wasi and the Polar Eskimos lived semi-nomadic lifestyles. It was the necessary means to obtaining food and/or water. Living permanently in one place would have depleted the available foodstuffs obtained by hunting and gathering. Agriculture of any kind was out of the question, prohibited by the climate. Climate was also the reason that the groups were semi-nomadic. The Eskimos traveled during hunting seasons but hunkered down to endure the frigid winters. The Ju/wasi camped out during the dry season to be close to a reliable water source without which they would die of dehydration. They traveled during the rainy season to get richer supplies of food. It would seem that this mobile lifestyle best suited small bands of men, women, and children numbering between two and three dozen individuals. Both the Eskimo and the Ju/wa groups were of this average. The economy of these people as related to their ability to feed the

group was wholly in terms of hunting and gathering. Their possessions were minimal and often limited to the implements necessary for survival, i.e. tools and clothing. Housing for the Ju/wasi was temporary, quickly assembled dome huts of twigs and grass which were abandoned when the group left. No one slept in the huts. They were more token than functional, a place to keep some few possessions. They also provided a bit of shade from the sun. The huts were never reoccupied. Winter houses for Eskimos were more durable structures of stone and earth. For the Ammassalik Eskimos they were communal property owned by no one. Each winter it was mutually agreed who would share which building, as each structure would often house several families.

As described by sociologists and anthropologists the economic unit of these societies was the husband and wife partnership. Both contributed to the union. Men in both societies hunted and provided animal carcasses which yielded meat, skins, and bones for tools. Men made tools as required, especially for hunting. In the case of the Eskimos animals were also the source of blubber which was an essential food and provided fuel for cooking and heating. Eskimo men hunted during the six or eight warmer months to supply enough meat for the duration of the coming winter months. Women were excluded from hunting so that they could raise children. This was a simple biological reality. Neither Eskimo men or Ju/wa men considered themselves better than women because they hunted. Eskimo men joked that they took on the strenuous tasks of hunting to keep their women beautiful.

Women in the Ju/wa society gathered root vegetables, berries, and nuts. They built the small grass huts. They prepared leather hides from animal skins. In the Eskimo society women fabricated clothing by preparing skins, designing and cutting the materials, and sewing the final garment. Women kept lamps aflame, cooked, and took care of domestic chores. The tasks necessary for survival and for raising a family were divided between husband and wife, but neither considered his or her position in the partnership to be of more value. Each knew that without the other partner they could not survive. In both societies the most important aspect of the community's economic well-being was the practice of sharing food among all. This was an absolute. Meat brought in from the hunt was carefully doled out. Distribution to each individual was performed according to precise customs, and everyone received a portion. Both Eskimo and Ju/wa societies had this practice, though the specific methods differed. In both societies these customs were also carefully designed to make sure that while the hunter who had actually made the kill was given due credit others had ways of being thanked for their contribution to the economic well-being of the group.

Group social structure
The Polar Eskimos and the Ju/wasi lived in small bands averaging 25 to 40 individuals. Their ethnic populations were small and spread over very large territories thousands of square miles in area. They moved about extensively and casually kept in touch with distant groups, sharing news and occasionally small gifts. Members of the group were often related which would seem normal in populations of less than 500 individuals, but one did not need kinship to be a part of the group. Group numbers and the general population were judiciously limited by natural birth rates. Group membership changed occasionally as individuals or couples and their offspring joined up with the group or left to travel with other bands. Everyone was ultimately familiar with the entire ethnic population. Men and women divided types of labor into what was suitable for each. Men and women shared equal social status, without obvious or subtle domination by either. No one in the entire society was subservient to anyone else. Children were an integral part of the groups and were not excluded or isolated. All adults were confident and independent minded. All individuals shared equal political status. Thus adults made decisions about their own circumstances. Decisions regarding the community were made through group discussion with tolerance and respect for all. Everyone participated in discussion until a unanimous agreement was reached. No one dictated decisions. No one held more influence than another. No one was held in higher regard than others. The people were naturally gregarious, friendly, and sociable. The group may have existed for economic reasons, as survival was easier when the individuals lived and worked together, but it also existed for social reasons. Everyone enjoyed each other's company and companionship. They chatted, joked, and visited with each other continually. The group had intimate knowledge of every member. All actions and emotions were open for the whole group to see.

There were no social rules or taboos in either society. People did not need to define proper behavior. People were considerate of all those around them. If someone made a faux pas, they were told about it. They would apologize and make amends, and that would be the end of it. When making decisions or solving problems individuals based their actions on what was best for the group. In fact they did not think of their friends and relatives as a group, but rather as the people they shared their lives with.

The societies stand out in negative comparison to modern cultures. The qualities of these two primitive societies are revealed more readily by what they were not. There was no political order or governing of any kind. No one gave orders. No one held power of any kind. There was no headman, no tribal chief, no shaman. There was no council of elders. There were no burial rites or death rituals. There was no religion. No one ritually worshipped or prayed to any supernatural deity or deities. The people were generally happy. In spite of the most difficult circumstances for survival no one despondently complained about hardship or the ill-fate of their lives. No one begged for forgiveness because there was nothing to be forgiven. There were no moral or ethical codes of conduct. All conduct was known to all. There was no attempt at privacy for the Ju/wasi. The Eskimos kept nothing secret from one another.

In terms of Margaret Mead's sociological analyses, both the Ju/wa and the Polar Eskimo societies, unlike most primitive and all Civilized societies, were cooperative not competitive. They worked together. They shared all tasks. They all contributed to taking care of the children. They discussed problems and agreed on solutions.

Family social structure

One of the more startling omissions of the two societies as far as modern sociology and popular opinion are concerned was the absence of marriage ceremonies or marriage vows. A man and a woman chose to be together and lived together. The reality of their union was obvious to all. Families might be informed beforehand, but it was not in the way of asking permission. A marriage union was not built upon notions of romantic love. It was an agreement between the man and the woman with strong underlaying economic reasons. A marriage union was not sacrosanct. If there should happen to be strong marital discord the two simply parted company, something that was quite rare. Husband and wife understood that survival in their world was best achieved by cooperative effort. Each knew their own responsibilities and the necessity of their spouse's efforts. Because of this understanding husband and wife were equal partners and deeply respected each other.

The societies as a whole were neither patriarchal nor matriarchal. Women gave birth no more frequently than one child every four or five years. Having more babies than that would severely hamper a woman's ability to raise the first child and to do all of her necessary work.

When a child was born there was no ceremony or celebration. Babies were continuously cared for by their mothers. During infancy the baby was carried by its mother and nursed as frequently as the baby wished. Even as a toddler was learning to walk it would be carried by its mother on foraging treks so as not to slow the group. The young child learned to hold onto its mother in such a way that the mother could walk and work hands-free. Babies were quiet, and children were well-behaved. All people were well-behaved. Kids didn't yell and scream or pester their parents, and parents didn't constantly reprimand their kids. Husbands and wives did not argue, and there was no spousal abuse.

There were no ceremonies or ritual bereavements when a member of the family or the group died.

Behavior

One might describe the behavior of these people, both the Eskimos and the Ju/wa bushmen as being "quite civilized". Which is really to say that they possessed anything but today's common behavior. They were respectful, friendly, and soft-spoken. They did not rant and rave about anything or anyone. They did not complain. They were good-natured and smiled more often than not. The people were non-competitive and nonaggressive in every aspect of their relationships with others. The members of the two societies showed no evidence of competitive games. No one ran faster than another. No one had skills better than another. One Ju/wa man might be a very good hunter, but he was never a better hunter. An Eskimo wife might sew exquisite clothing, but it was never better clothing than someone else had done. When children played they did not form teams or win victories over others. They merely took turns playing at the same thing.

These simple hunter-gatherers were open and unassuming. Eskimo people were self-deprecating in their speech. They did not use their names or first-person pronouns when speaking. Ju/wasi were exceedingly humble and took no credit or praise for what they did. The people of both cultures were courageous and had no irrational fears. Ju/wa men confronted lions, though they would not hunt them in a mutual unspoken truce between the two species. Eskimo men armed only with hand-thrown spears and needing to get within yards of the animal went up against formidable polar bears that could weigh as much as 1,000 pounds. The members of both societies lived in small close-knit communities under difficult conditions. Life was not easy, and there certainly was opportunity for stress to build in an individual or amongst the group. As is the case with any successful human community practices existed to assuage the straining of emotions. Polar Eskimos enjoyed sex with multiple partners, sharing husbands and wives without secrecy. The Ju/wasi would spontaneously initiate a communal dance that could last eight or ten hours into the dawn of the next day. Both peoples displayed good senses of humor and wit. They joked and kidded genially. A prosperous hunt was always celebrated as a community in jubilant fashion.

They were non-confrontational not only within their close-knit societies, but in response to intrusions from outside. When an aggressive herdsman from a neighboring tribe usurped a Ju/wasi waterhole by bringing his cattle to graze there, the Ju/wasi moved on and relinquished the site. The Ju/wasi hunted with poisoned arrows and could easily have reclaimed the spot but did not do so. Polar Eskimos forgave the rude and insulting behaviors of European explorers and traders with the understanding that the Europeans had not developed maturity or wisdom to understand life.

Intellect

The Polar Eskimos and the Kalahari Ju/wa bushmen were very intelligent and clever. They were capable and confident. They would not have survived if they had not been so. They were illiterate and had no knowledge of written language. However, they could read every nuance in every detail of their environments. They had absolute knowledge of all plants, birds, animals, and insects that lived within the thousands of square miles that were their world. The Ju/wasi knew individual trees and waterholes and gullies that would fill with water during the rainy season. Eskimos navigated hundreds of miles over an almost featureless, often completely white landscape. Skills were learned in both societies simply by careful observation. The young imitated the adults. Neither formal education nor prolonged and detailed verbal instruction was a part of their life experience. Thinking for these people was pragmatic. They reasoned problems and evaluated choices with the sole criterion of efficient survival. They had no beliefs in supernatural people, places, or things. They lived day to day without wishful thinking or abstract philosophical meanderings. Their musings were not about the why's of life. They did not ask why human beings were on this planet, or why the sky was blue, or why the sun came up in the East in the morning and went down in the West at night. They rather pondered the practical how's of life. They asked themselves how best to approach an eland or a polar bear standing in an open rocky terrain, or how does a root ripen over time, or how would an antelope skin or seal skin be most effectively put to use. There were no eternal truths to be pondered. They concerned themselves with the moment and the seasons ahead. Individuals of both cultures declared how beautiful and bountiful were the worlds in which they lived.

Both the Ju/wasi and the Eskimos sang and played music. The Ju/wasi sang on various occasions and were sometimes accompanied by any of several types of handmade stringed instruments. The Eskimos fabricated drums by stretching skins over bone frameworks. Both societies used songs as a method of social mediation. When a rare dispute became evident among the Eskimos the two antagonists would beseech each other at a public "drum-song" in which each would sing in turn and express their grievances. This usually sufficed to end the matter. Elizabeth Marshall Thomas described an event in which two Ju/wa women had an ongoing argument, and the rest of the small band began the practice of singing a song about them whenever their tempers flared. The women were so embarrassed by their unseemly behavior in front of others, by losing their self control, that they ceased the quarreling.

When people told stories or fables the characters were the animals in their world. They did not have oral histories or stories of great events or human heroes. Stories were told for entertainment.

Neither the Ju/wasi nor the Eskimos created graphic or symbolic art.

The 99%
Such is the description of two representative simple hunter-gatherer peoples. Analysis of the facts reveals that the members of these societies lacked any motivations or behaviors that could be called self-centered. Nor were their worlds anthropocentric. The people did not separate themselves from nature. They did not feel that nature or the world around them was antagonistic in any way. They did not feel that they struggled for survival. They were simply living their lives as was required.

It should be evident that people untouched by Civilization were different from us. Their societies functioned differently, without rules or structure. Their personalities and behaviors were different, without aggression or selfishness or egotism. They lacked all of the assumed prerequisites for any human society: leadership, rituals for marriage and death, social hierarchy, and religion.

It is a 99% flip. It is a 99% difference in lifestyles, a 99% difference in perception of self, and a 99% difference in social behaviors. The 1% of discord amongst the Eskimos or the Ju/wasi is evidence that they were subject to human foibles. The 1% of goodness and selflessness in Civilized societies is evidence that we are capable of better behaviors. But it cannot be denied that 99% cooperative became 99% competitive. It cannot be denied that 99% naive unawareness of self became 99% egocentric.

The Polar Eskimos and the Kalahari Ju/wasi lived as they had lived for thousands of years before being confronted with Modern Civilization. It is not unreasonable to postulate that the simple hunter-gatherers of 150,000 years of prehistory were of the same character.

Magus Figure from
La Grotte de Trois Frères

4. Change

We know that an art style which had endured 20,000 years of consistency disappeared and was replaced by art styles so completely different that we must ask how and why this happened. Art had been realistic. It had portrayed animals and ignored human beings. It had not portrayed emotion or dynamic action. It had not been narrative, commemorative, or didactic. It had been inspired by visual clues in the shadows of lamplight on cave walls. Art associated with known Civilizations is completely different: anthropocentric, abstract representational, and dramatic. It is inspired by intellectual cues from within the mind.

We know that for 150,000 years during the Paleolithic era human societies were different from societies today. They were semi-nomadic and survived by hunting and foraging. Judging by accounts of hunter-gatherers such as the Polar Eskimos and the Kalahari Ju/wasi our prehistoric ancestors were simpler. They lived cooperatively and openly with each other. They lived as equals among equals. They lived without rules of any kind. They lived without introspection, philosophy, or knowledge of Good and Evil. They lived happily without self-awareness or ego.

We know what history has told us about human lifestyle and behaviors over the past 6,000 years. The 6,000 year history of Western Civilization shows scorched trails of human exploits across the world. From the fertile valleys of the Tigris, Euphrates, and Nile rivers Civilization flickered westward along the shores of the Mediterranean. Over slow millennia Mesopotamian and Egyptian hotspots gave way to glowing embers in Greece and then Rome. Roman influence charred the British Isles, smudged all of North Africa, encircled the Black Sea; then cooled. Later, Islam sent another surge of Civilization from the Middle East through the northern African continent and Spain. Christian Civilization smoldered until it caught flame during the Renaissance. Then European nations burst forth to convert and colonize the Americas, the whole of Africa, India, Australia, and South East Asia. In China and India Civilizations had waxed and waned for thousands of years. Advances in communications technology ultimately melted all peoples and cultures into our Modern amalgam of a Civilized global community.

This igniting of history is a relatively benign image of Civilization's conquests during the six millennia of history. It maps the expansions of educated cultures throughout the lands. Civilization has also been responsible for seemingly endless plunder and destruction that ravaged entire populations of human beings. The notable cultures mentioned above certainly used violence and domination as the primary means of spreading influence. There were other myriad wildfires by barbarian humanity that left nothing but ash. Annihilative Goths, Huns, Slavs, and Mongols were no less Civilized.

The most obvious thing revealed by this blink-of-an-eye look at 6,000 years of history is that there were lots of people, millions of people, aggressive people everywhere.

What is the composition of history? What is it that men have recorded of themselves? What has been notable and newsworthy enough to be memorable?

Most of history is about power and domination. History is generally given as a linear sequence of military wars and political control. It is the genealogy of dynasties and kingdoms and empires. Egyptians under Ramses II fought Hittites at Kadesh. Spartans defied Xerxes' Persians at Thermopylae. Alexander the Great conquered Civilizations from the Adriatic to the Indus. Hannibal of Carthage tested the power of Rome only to be defeated by Scipio Africanus at Zama. Attila's Huns invaded the Balkans, Gaul, and Italy. Harold was defeated by William the Conqueror at the Battle of Hastings. Genghis Khan's Mongol Empire was the largest ever to have been established. Napoleon unified Europe until his final defeat at Waterloo. Grant defeated Lee at Appomattox effectively ending the American Civil War. World War II ended when Hitler's Third Reich was defeated after the Allies under General Eisenhower undertook the Normandy Invasion.

History is driven by conflict and wars and the warriors that fought them. It is enacted by charismatic, forceful, and/or lucky men. The progression of history through time has always been pushed by individuals. Every battle and every war recorded is accompanied by the names of generals, kings, and heroes who gained fame during the bloody conflicts. Adventurers seeking fame and fortune found their places in history. Scientists, scholars, holy men, artists, and philosophers fill historic accounts. Murders, liars, cheats, usurpers, and idiots walk the same pages of history.

Scandalous courtesans, shrewd women of uncommon beauty, and formidable queens are not ignored by history. Through 6,000 years of history these personages have been recognized as memorable. They characterize humanity. But they do not characterize the humanity that existed in prehistory more than 10,000 years ago. The skills and personalities these men and women possessed, the skills and personalities that made them famous or infamous in the recorded story of mankind were skills and personalities that had nothing to do with biological or evolutional survival. These people are only remarkable in the context of Civilization.

Most people of history were motivated by power, wealth, domination, and fame. Many had only personal ambitions and sought aggrandizement above all else. They wanted as much as possible while they lived and wanted legacies and monumental tombs after they were dead. Other people of history were motivated by ideas, ideals, and beliefs. They pledged their lives to religion, to romantic love, to patriotism, to justice, and to truth. They believed that death was not an end, that Good triumphs over Evil, that superior people should help those less fortunate; that ideas were worth dying for.

Not one thing in the history of Civilization has precedence in early prehistory: not the motivations, not the ideas, not the beliefs.

History has always assumed that there are absolutes about every human society. Among those absolutes are leadership, religion, social hierarchies, social taboos, marriage, and commemoration of a person's dying. Even the most primitive human clan or group needed a headman or shaman, an alpha male to make decisions and keep order. Every human society had a form of religion with recognition of Supernatural gods, spirits, and demons. No society could function without social order in the form of rules and forbidden taboos. Social class or familial rank provided necessary structure and organization. The recognition of a man and a woman uniting for life with solemn and joyous ceremony was natural. Similarly, observing the passing of a family member and close friend from this life into the next was equally natural, an emotional and psychological necessity. Yet none of these things existed in early prehistory, not in the simplest or most elemental form.

History is profoundly and absolutely anthropocentric. It is about human beings and nothing else. If there should be a reference to any other biological species it is only as that species relates to the affairs of mankind. If there is mention of volcanic eruptions, of torrential monsoons, or of enduring drought, it is only as these natural phenomena relate to human endeavor. Simple hunter-gatherers such as our prehistoric ancestors lived without awareness of self or human segregation from the rest of the natural world.

History is the biographical record of humanity. But it is only the biographical record of recent generations of men and women. It has required written words and written numbers. Such written symbols are abstract representation, a unique ability of the human mind. There is evidence of abstract representation in the form of graphic tectiforms found in the same caves as the prehistoric paintings of animals. Identical symbols can be found in a number of caves. There are relatively few of these scribblings. It would seem that prehistoric people were intellectually capable of symbolic representation. But it was not something that they pursued. It was not something they gave much effort to.

Oral histories have been noticed among many illiterate societies. Even without symbolic representation people have kept the memory of extraordinary events, noteworthy individuals, and family genealogies. Passing along such accounts from generation to generation requires considerable effort. For more than 150,000 years people had no concern for remembering what had happened to their forebears. Simple hunter-gatherer societies had no oral histories. They had no accounts of wonderfully unique individuals, of heroic acts, or of remarkable events.

It is more than obvious that about 10,000 years ago something about the character of human beings changed radically. People became self-centered, aggressive, judgmental, and competitive. How did the culture and personality of mankind undergo such a complete metamorphosis?

Let us piece together what we know and can logically assume. It can be assumed because we know the final result.

We know Civilization is about 10,000 years old. Human Civilization has left ample physical evidence. There are structural ruins of cities that were economically supported by agriculture. They have storage bins for grains, communal refuse heaps, and penned enclosures for domesticated animals. There are decorated pottery shards, painted murals, clay imprints of woven textiles, and tools unique to farming. Civilization originated in these expanding agricultural communities.

So what happened between 12,000 years ago, when we still had a few artists painting horses and bison and bulls in caves, and 10,000 years ago when Civilization began to appear in structured cities?

Twelve thousand years ago the Last Ice Age receded and global climate changed. Polar ice sheets that had covered northern Europe and Canada and Siberia with glacial ice one mile thick melted. Ocean levels rose 400 feet, and shorelines diminished to what we know today. The global climate system changed. Temperatures rose dramatically. Rainfall increased. Ocean currents changed. Wind patterns changed.

In response to climate changes the land environments and biomes changed. Treeless tundra plains in northern France became temperate forests. Desert expanses across the globe became fertile and green. Plant life thrived with increased growth and increased variety. Natural grain fields filled valleys. Animal life underwent shocking changes. The megafauna that had inhabited Europe for more than 40,000 years disappeared. Mammoths and wooly rhinos died out. Bison and reindeer relocated. Ibex moved to higher, cooler mountain slopes. Species altered, adapted, and multiplied. Woodland, steppe, and savannah animal populations increased.

With the increase in plant and animal populations human beings had more abundant food sources. They did not have to travel so far to obtain suitable nutrition. They found that they could live in more permanent locations, especially locations beside fertile lowlands where there was an abundant and consistent supply of cereal grains. Men still hunted for meat, but there were enough herd animals on the grassy plains so that they need not search too far.

We can rationally assume that women soon realized that certain new types of vine vegetables could be transplanted and grown closer to home. Men learned how to increase production of grains simply by clearing more land. Women and men judiciously harvested and stored plant foods.

Eventually human beings realized that they would not have to hunt for meat if they could raise animals close to home. Goats, pigs, sheep, cattle, and chickens were captured and domesticated. Men no longer needed to leave home to hunt game. This allowed for year-round permanent housing, and human societies were freed from nomadic and semi-nomadic lifestyles.

We know that human societies started living in cities and that the numbers of people living together was greater than had ever been before.

We know that Çatal Huyuk was an agricultural city with more than 3,000 people. There is evidence of domesticated livestock. There was storage of grain. Each domicile had bins and jars for storing food. There were specialized tools for harvesting and threshing grains. There were ovens and utensils for preparing food for the new diet.

Three thousand inhabitants lived in Çatal Huyuk. The Polar Eskimos and the Kalahari Ju/wasi each had populations of less than 500 individuals spread out over thousands of square miles. They lived in bands of between 25 and 35 men, women, and children. The Polar Eskimos and Ju/wasi lived as human populations had lived for 150,000 years. Population density had been limited, checked, and in balance with the natural environment. But the ruins of Çatal Huyuk reveal what had happened to humanity over a few thousand years. It was not the only city flourishing at the time, and people had certainly not come from two continents to huddle together. The number of human beings living on Planet Earth had multiplied exponentially.

Factors relevant to the advent of Civilized human societies are agriculture, sedentary living, and population growth. But agriculture and sedentary living are really only factors because they led to increased populations.

How did human populations increase so dramatically in a few thousand years? Populations had been limited for 150,000 years. What changed? It would seem fairly obvious that available food supplies played a role. Without an abundance of food an increase in population could not be sustained. But an abundance of nutritional resources was not cause enough.

For 150,000 years the mechanism of population balance had been engineered by lifestyle. It was not simply a biological response to available food supply. It was not a conscious intellectual decision. Populations had been naturally kept in check by simple hunter-gatherer societies because a woman gave birth to no more than one child every four or five years. It was a practical necessity. A mother could not take care of more than one child at a time. She carried a young baby constantly. She nursed an infant for more than two years, sometimes four. She hauled a toddler around when she went foraging, sometimes many miles away. It was impractical to have children more frequently. It was a burden on the whole community. Even if more food was available it was not practical for a nomadic or semi-nomadic group to support additional children. This was common sense and natural.

When human societies settled into permanent dwellings women were freed from many of the former limitations and worries of caring for babies and toddlers. Fixed housing offered security. Sedentary lifestyles meant that mothers did not have to carry their children on foraging treks or seasonal relocation. The result of all of this change was that a husband and wife did not have to wait four or five years to have additional children. If there was sufficient food, having a child every one, two, or three years was not out of the question. It was certainly biologically possible.

The transition to farming subsistence was no doubt gradual. But at some point sedentary agriculture usurped the semi-nomadic hunter-gatherer lifestyle that had persisted for 150,000 years. Populations blossomed.

The little stick men running rampant in hunting scene paintings found at Çatal Huyuk show that by 9,000 years ago something had changed in the human mind. Polished obsidian mirrors were among the excavated artifacts. For what purpose? The human mind also thought that there was some significance to installing animal skulls covered with plaster on the interior walls of a house. All of this is very significant.

It reveals that the Seed of Civilization had taken hold.

Why did the character and personalities of all human beings undergo a Dr. Jekyll – Mr. Hyde transformation? Why did cooperative, non-aggressive homo sapiens become competitive, confrontational, Civilized men? Did they became greedy when confronted by the prospect of possessions and wealth? Did they become lazy and think it easier to steal food instead of finding it in an abundant nature?

Warfare, crime, kings, religion, wealth, and social hierarchies are entangled in Civilization. None of these things was the catalyst that encouraged Civilization to grow. None of these things was the root cause of Civilization. They are all symptomatic.

Civilization grew and took root because there were no longer checks on population growth. Surprisingly, it was not the burgeoning growth of the human population per se that initiated the Civilizing of man. It was the increase in human birthrate that gave flower to the Seed of Civilization. It did not matter how many children a woman bore. What mattered was the spacing of those children. The fact that a mother could give birth to another child while her first was still younger than three years old changed the character of mankind.

5. The Psychological Shift

For 150,000 years human beings were good-natured hunter-gatherers. Then, for the past 10,000 years Civilized men redefined mankind as an invasive, war-mongering scourge of the earth. What switch was thrown? What wrench was tossed into the clockwork mechanism of human evolution? How could the whole homo sapiens species go from a seeming lack of self-awareness to an anthropocentric brave new world?

The advent of Civilization was not revealed by changes in architecture or new tool technologies or in personal possessions. Civilization was evinced by changes in behavior and changes in personality. People changed.

If people changed, how do we academically analyze people? How do we academically analyze changes in behavior and changes in personality? Anthropology and sociology describe them, but they do not go beyond observation.

What is the legitimate study of personality?

It is psychology.

As much as scientists would like to believe otherwise, human nature is not defined by biology. Simple hunter-gatherers are the obvious proof. They were socially non-aggressive. They lived cooperatively without competition. They had no alpha males or chieftains to lead them. Modern Civilized human beings with the same biology are the antithesis of every behavior exhibited by hunter-gatherers.

As a species we do not kill other people because of biology. We do not scream and abuse other people because of biology. We do not get married because of biology.

No, human nature is not defined by biology. Human nature is defined by psychology.

Psychology is considered by many to be a pseudo-science. It is a new understanding to human thinking. Sigmund Freud is credited with introducing it some 120 years ago. Its original motivation and much of its focus have been on the analysis of abnormal psychologies, the antisocial behaviors and neurotic mental illnesses that plague certain individuals. It took half a century before psychologists considered defining parameters for normal psychological profiles and normal psychological developments. Only in the past few decades has it begun to concern itself with other

aspects of brain function such as cognitive awareness and learning mechanisms.
Psychology still has a stigma in academic circles and popular opinion. Yet we use its principles and concepts daily. Ego, obsessive-compulsive, control freak, passive-aggressive, megalomaniac, sibling rivalry, inferiority complex, and subliminal suggestion are terms known, understood, and accepted by most of us. They are all concepts acquired from the study of psychology. They seem to be evident and obvious when given a word to describe behaviors we readily perceive.

For all of its strangeness and inability to substantiate many of its theories, the study of psychology ranks with evolution, plate tectonics, and particle physics as one of the great understandings established in the past 200 years. It has given us insight into the broadest spectrum of personal and societal behaviors.

The Psychological Development of the Human Infant

Psychology does not define us. It does not create us. It is a developmental process beginning at birth that allows us to function throughout our lives. Psychology is the vehicle by which we relate to others and to the world. It is part emotion and part thought-processing. It is the foundation for our behaviors. Psychological development is unique to each person born into this life. However, it does have definable aspects common to all.

In the first decade of the 20th century it was Freud who postulated that early childhood held the sources of most human neuroses. He defined ego as an individual's self image. Ego developed at an early age and remained a strong psychological motivator throughout life. Early childhood experiences influenced personality and behavior without an individual's conscious awareness.

In the 1950's Erik Erikson defined eight stages of personality development during a person's lifetime. The first stage upon which all others were dependent occurred from birth to six months of age and required the development of a bond of trust between the young infant and its mother. Without this bond the infant could never be sure of consistent patterns of social behaviors or physical actions. The second stage occurred from 2 to 3 years of age and required a toddler to gain confidence in its own physical abilities without which the child would suffer self-doubt and shame. The other six stages were age-related social struggles and were ultimately dependent upon success in the first two stages.

In the 1960's and 1970's John Bowlby and Mary Ainsworth defined an "Attachment" theory based on experimental observations. It stated that a secure attachment bond between a mother and an infant was necessary for the child's healthy psychological development. The bond was dependent not only on the infant receiving physical care and nourishment but also on an emotional interplay between mother and child. Without such a secure attachment a growing child could falter and possibly give up its will to live.

In 1975 Margret S. Mahler published *The Psychological Development of the Human Infant*. Her experimental research into child psychosis had created the need for a control group that would define normal childhood development. After a decade of studies she developed the theory of Separation-Individuation, a psychological development process during the first several years of every human being's life. It describes the development of self-awareness and identity within a child and the establishing of independence from its mother. It is the most elemental foundation for every individual's personality.

"*The biological birth of the human infant and the psychological birth of the individual are not coincident in time. The former is a dramatic, observable, and well-circumscribed event; the latter a slowly unfolding intrapsychic process.*" - Margret S. Mahler[1]

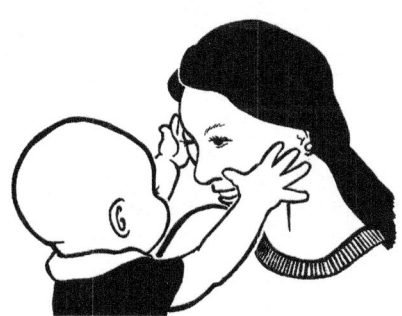

The Separation-Individuation Process

What Mahler had given verbal definition to is the experience every Modern child has of learning to let go of mother and to face the world on its own. That experience requires creating an inner core of self identity, an ego. It also requires the creation of a workable model of what is outside of oneself. These are the foundations for interaction with other people, with the physical world, and with events that will befall one in the course of living life. The whole process is done without guidance or sure knowledge or established method. It is working blind. An infant's mother is the only verity.

Margaret S. Mahler defined the Separation-Individuation process from observational data. The principal period of the S-I process is from 4 or 5 months to 30 or 36 months of age, but it goes on throughout one's lifetime and is never finished. It follows after a symbiotic period between newborn and mother, and involves achieving the ability to function separately from mother (separation) and achieving a unique personality of individual characteristics (individuation). The Separation-Individuation process is a prerequisite for the development of a sense of identity. The S-I process is a pre-verbal, pre-symbolic happening. It is thus completely subconscious in its machinations.

A newborn will experience two preliminary developmental phases before the S-I process begins. At birth and for the next two months an infant is in a Normal Autistic State: sleeping or only half awake, only subconsciously perceiving outside stimulus, and in its own self-contained world. As it gains sensory awareness it becomes aware of Mother's caring for its every physical and emotional need and enters the Normal Symbiotic State. The infant behaves as if it and its mother are a single entity. The infant is in a symbiotic relationship with its mother. The psychological definition of symbiosis is a state of un-differentiation, a fusion of the individual (as infant) with its mother. It is the time from birth when the infant is unable to differentiate a self as "I" from something that is separate and "not-I". Mother's face is the first true perception. The relationship with one's mother is the basis for all subsequent human relationships.

The actual Separation-Individuation process begins with the Differentiation phase. At four to five months a baby has become aware of the mother, half of its symbiotic oneness, as evidenced by a smiling response to mother. The infant is more wakeful and experiences longer periods of alertness and attention to external stimuli. At the same time it begins to notice the leaving and returning of its mother. This precipitates an awareness of mother as separate. The infant seeks a greater understanding of mother, leaning away instead of snuggling into mother's body and exploring tactile and visual information from mother's face and body. At seven to eight months the infant visually compares mother with other persons or things and then carefully compares with all senses. During this phase as a child gains motor capabilities it may slide off mother's lap and stand beside her, but it clings and holds on rather than moving away. There is also a checking back pattern, looking back to mother after looking away at some object or person.

Phase Two of the S-I process is Practicing. It is defined by the infant's physical development and acquisition of locomotive skills. Crawling, climbing, and standing allow the infant to physically separate itself from its mother. The entire process of learning to walk is a critical development in the mother-child relationship. Walking results in rapid body differentiation from mother. It helps establish a specific bond with mother. Walking also allows the growth of the infant's ego in close proximity to mother. Interest in mother expands to interest in inanimate objects. The infant's ability to roam about gives opportunity to explore more of the world around it. Mother remains the central focus, but the world is gradually experienced in ever-widening circles. The infant's contact with and comfort from its mother is the reassurance that enables such curiosity. Mother is the lighthouse in a storm of unknown.

The Separation-Individuation process is so named because there are two intertwined developments occurring at the same time. During this Practicing phase the duality of the process becomes evident. Separation is a defining of objects and reality outside the self. It is guided by the connection an infant has with its mother. Individuation is the creation of an ego, an image of self. That image of one's self will be continually augmented and adjusted throughout a lifetime. The creation of one's ego is greatly enhanced by the visual perspective that standing and walking allow. The infant's growing physical skills, its ability to perceive the world around it, and its sense of discovery all exhilarate the infant's growing autonomous ego to a peak of self-centeredness.

The third phase of the S-I process is Rapprochement, or bringing together; reconciliation. Having begun a certain physical independence during the Practicing phase, the infant, now a toddler, seeks to establish an optimal distance from/with mother. There is coercive behavior towards the mother alternating with desperate clinging to her. There is the beginning of a relationship to the father. This phase is one of heightened emotional struggles as belief in mother's omnipotence seems shaken. There is separation anxiety and a fear of losing mother's love. There is a seeking of parental approval. Separation anxiety must be dealt with and resolved. The emotional crises experienced during this phase of Rapprochement will in the future effect the quantity and the quality of stress traumas and the development confrontations during adolescence. This third phase is preceded by walking and by the cognitive development which attains speech and symbolic play. It is the first level of having a self identity, of being a unique individual. With the growing ability to be separate from mother there is an increased need for the reassurance of mother's love, for her physical presence, and for acceptance by mother. Speech and play become tools of these reassurances.

At 15 months mother is recognized as a separate person. The toddler wants to share its new findings and interesting things with mother. The child brings things to mother and seeks her equal interest in these things. This results in a realization that mother has a mind of her own and has likes and dislikes not always shared by the toddler. This can be very difficult emotionally for the child. During this phase the child's expanding social awareness is primarily evidenced by interacting with father. The child finds pleasure in being able to communicate with mother and others. At 18 months the child has experienced some life separate from mother and is quite taken with itself – with its new physical abilities of mobility, talking, and discovering new sensory data; and with its capabilities while all on its own. This new feeling of freedom and independence creates stress as the infant is directly or indirectly reminded that it still requires assistance from mother. Thus arises an internal conflict of emotions towards mother – wanting her attention and sense of security but pushing and turning away from her in anger as an expression of frustrated independence. These mood swings of needing and rejecting mother are often from one minute to the next. Stress and anxiety increase, resulting in indecision and a nonacceptance of strangers.

During this phase the child will accept another as symbolic replacement of mother in a favorable way and/or will angrily substitute another to express the displeasure of mother's absence. At 21 months there is finally an easing of tension and struggle by finding an optimal distance from mother where the child can feel independent but still secure in the knowledge that the support of mother is near. This enables the child to have individual expression and control. Achieving optimal distance is made possible by using language, by fantasy play, and by understanding rules. Language allows the child to feel a sense of control by naming objects and expressing wants. The use of the word "I" develops at this time. The Separation-Individuation process includes self-aggrandizing as the child becomes aware of its ability to control objects and of its ability to determine the outcome of actions.

The final phase of the S-I process is given the descriptive name of Preliminary Libidinal Object Constancy. The phase occurs between 25 and 36 months. During this time the child achieves a certain degree of emotional object constancy with regard to mother and also achieves a definite individuality. The internalization of the love object, i.e. mother, stabilizes the infant's emotional need and allows for longer and easier separation from mother. This fourth phase is open-ended, only beginning a sometimes lifelong process. The process is also not linear since achieving a certain degree of constancy can be undone, with progress slipping backwards and sometimes lost. Physical object constancy of material things in the child's environment occurs earlier and is different from the emotional object constancy of the love object which takes longer to establish through symbolic internalizing of the mother's image. During this phase a developing sense of time makes it easier to be without the mother. Continuing speech development allows for greater self-expression and thus individuality. Mental images of self as separate from mother allow for complete ego formation. During the second half of the third year, from 30 to 36 months, there is no longer the need for immediate satisfaction, and the child's emotional equilibrium is maintained in spite of mother's temporary absences.

That is a quick summation of the Separation-Individuation process as put forth by Margret S. Mahler. It is obvious that the first few years of everyone's life are a caldron of emotion-filled anxieties. At birth an infant is brought into a situation it has been ill prepared for. The infant's mother is its rock and anchor providing nourishment and stability. But the child soon learns it must find its own way. It is that initial struggle to face and deal with the unknown that colors each human psyche for the rest of life.

As R. Buckminster Fuller stated it, *"All humanity has always been born naked, absolutely helpless for months... no experience, therefore absolutely ignorant. That is the way all humanity has always started... [Man] having then no rule book, nothing to tell him about that Universe, has had to find his way entirely by trial and error."* [2]

Yes, that is the way all humanity has always started. But for 150,000 years it was a little easier. Well, no. It was much easier.

An Archaic SI Process

The birthrate in both the Ju/wa and the Eskimo societies was not the same as it is in today's world. A woman did not give birth more frequently than once every four or five years. Connecting this fact about reproduction with Mahler's Separation-Individuation process, there is an awareness that children who lived before 10,000 years ago underwent the three year S-I process with two extremely important differences from Modern children.

First, infants who underwent the Separation-Individuation process more than 10,000 years ago experienced that process in closer proximity to their mothers than do Modern infants. Closer proximity might be considered an understatement. Their mothers were with them constantly. The infant was always within reach. A mother never lost sight of or concern for her child. This continuous care lasted for at least the first several years and often four or five.

Secondly, children of nomadic and semi-nomadic societies experienced the S-I process without close siblings. If children are born too close to each other there will be conflict. Young siblings are in constant need of their mothers. Two or three infants who are fully dependent on a single, nourishing mother create an undeniable demand on the mother. She cannot provide affection and physical care for all whenever they seek it. The children will be deprived, both physically and emotionally, of the complete nurturing that they desperately need at this time in their lives. Ultimately caught in a struggle for survival a child needs to compete with its brother or sister for mother's attention. Psychologists recognize this competition as Sibling Rivalry.

The differences of the enduring closeness to mother and the absence of sibling rivalry are enough to warrant a revision of Mahler's theory of the psychological development of the human infant. There is, in fact, an Archaic SI process that describes the psychological growth of human infants during the 150,000 years of prehistory, and there is a Modern Separation-Individuation process which describes the psychological progression of all human beings since then. The physical circumstances in each provide two very different incubations for the growing psyche.

The Archaic SI process was experienced by a growing infant in a wholly supportive environment. The baby that started life in a symbiotic relationship with its mother remained in that shared closeness for a much longer time than do today's infants. Mothers did not leave their infants unattended for any time for fear of natural dangers and predators. The child was never without the security of constant physical contact with the mother who carried the infant slung to her body, nursed the infant whenever required, and held the child on her back or in her lap when sitting. The baby slept with its body against its mother. The infant nursed at its mother's breast for three, four, or even more years. Closeness was not limited to the first six months of an infant's life. It continued for years, until the child was fully capable of keeping up with adults when traveling.

"[Ju/wa] babies are carried most of the time by their mothers, tied in soft leather slings against their mother's side, where they can easily reach their mother's breast. They nurse at will. [Ju/wa] women have excellent lactation. All *babies are plump. The babies wear no clothes and are skin-to-skin with their mothers. They sleep in their mother's arms at night. When they are not in their mother's arms or tied to their sides, they are in someone else's arms, or if they are set down to play they clamber over their elders as they lie chatting and resting, or play within arm's reach. The babies are constantly in the presence of people who are gentle and affectionate with them and who are watchful."* [3]

The Separation-Individuation process observed and defined by Dr. Mahler and her associates begins as the child gains a visual awareness of mother's going and returning. It may be postulated that in the Archaic SI process this development of visual awareness was not in regard to the coming and going of mother because it was begun from the vantage point of being actually physically attached to mother and looking outward. Mother rarely left. A sense of being separate from mother, which is a primary foundation of the Modern S-I process, may not have been the first understanding which contributed to the individual's identity. In the Archaic SI process the symbiotic closeness with mother extended throughout most of the several years of the early psychological growth period and may never have been lost per se. In the Modern S-I process the loss of the symbiotic relation with mother occurs as early as six months and certainly within the first year.

It should also be noted that emergence of physical motor skills plays a large part in the second Practicing phase of the Modern S-I process. A child uses its increasing abilities to crawl, walk, and run to journey ever farther away from mother and then return. This adventurous daring reinforces the individual's ego but needs the security of returning to mother. It is a very emotional tug-of-war balancing courage and confidence against the fear of losing the only known source ensuring survival. At this early age the child feels the need to explore the world on its own and to learn how it works. But it does not have the intellectual or physical abilities to do so. This phase is a time of angst and dilemma and feelings of insecurity. It is doubtful that such an emotional roller-coaster was experienced in the Archaic process.

It is interesting to see that Elizabeth Marshall Thomas considered the experience of carrying young Ju/wa children worth relating. She noted that the children used their strength and agility to climb onto and cling to whomever was carrying them. They did not require being held. They were not being carried by their mothers so much as going along for the ride. The infants quickly became less of a physical burden. This was a tremendous help to their mothers. The children's improving physical motor skills were used to reinforce their relationship with their mothers, not to attempt to separate themselves from their mothers. By coordinating their efforts with their caregivers they strengthened the original symbiotic partnership.

The Archaic SI process by which the infant eventually was weaned from mother's care was a slow gentle progression. It lacked the trauma of the Modern Separation-Individuation process. Mother was ever-present. She taught and guided the infant in its growing awareness of the world around. The infant was able to enter this world with the confidence and assurance gained from a complete psychological knowledge of mother's support even as the child eventually stepped away from her physically. When the infant did separate itself from its mother it moved into the secure psychological environment of sociable human beings. All helped each other with the understanding that cooperation and sharing were the best ways for individual and group to thrive. The child never went into the world feeling that it would need to struggle alone for survival. Psychologically, what had begun as a symbiotic relationship with mother was never abandoned as in the Modern S-I process but was rather expanded to include the entire band or tribe of people dwelling in the geographic neighborhood. Throughout its life the child would have a secure psychological attachment to mother and all of its human kin. It is also very possible that early human beings did not recognize a separation from the rest of the natural world, that the symbiotic relationship extended to include all of nature.

The Archaic SI process by which the infant acquired an understanding of its identity as a unique being was very different from the Modern procedure. In both Archaic and Modern procedures an infant must define itself by comparison with other living things it experiences. In the Archaic process of defining itself the infant looked at all that was around it. It observed animate and noted inanimate. All of the five senses were employed in the process. It understood the physical laws that characterized life on this planet. It noted the nature of inanimate objects, what forces would effect change and with what resistance. It recognized itself as an animate being and fit itself into the categories of behavior it observed in other living creatures. The infant noted consistencies and patterns of behavioral response. It observed social and functional interactions of the other human beings. The infant did all of this from a vantage point of security. Observation was an intellectual, unemotional evaluation.

In contrast, the dual nature of the Modern Separation-Individuation process is torture and torment to a new human being. The Modern Separation procedure is initiated by the infant subconsciously becoming aware that its source for all safety, caring, and sustenance may not be reliable over the long haul. The child never has the opportunity to passively observe. It places itself in full aggressive interaction with its environment when it tries to learn how to survive independent of mother. It goes into the world with trepidation and bewilderment. Its knowledge is accidental, often misdirected, experimentation.

Margaret S. Mahler stated an important observation in her studies. *"In these children disturbed symbiosis was not caused by indifference or depression on the part of the mother, but by her unpredictability."*[4] It was the unpredictability of mother's actions which caused the infant to believe he or she could not rely on mother in the symbiotic relationship. It is not the loss of an emotional support or communicated unhappiness that arouses trauma. It is the loss of the physical presence and constancy of mother. Mother's casual depositing of the child and then visually and even audibly leaving the child's immediate vicinity gives the child sufficient concern. It cannot see her or hear her. Its brain has not yet acquired enough knowledge of this world to know if she still exists when she is not physically perceived. She has disappeared. Even if she returns it has become a possibility that at some time she might not come back.

If there is a brother or sister on the scene, the clues of impending abandonment are more obvious. A mother's conflict of interest in the presence of a needy sibling is a warning to the developing young psyche that it might need to fend for itself. Another mouth to feed means less for the first child. Another crying baby means mother is not always free to answer its needs.

With this understanding of an insecure future the infant attempts to accept the inevitable need to go out on its own, separating itself from mother because of perceived necessity. This is not an easy step to take, and the child is caught in the excitement and anxiety of leaving and returning, conflicting necessities. Separation from mother is not something the infant wants to do. It would certainly prefer the comfort of mother's arms. But the child knows it must survive, and it courageously attempts to do just that. So it tries to experience the world on its own with the intent of learning how to exist as a single unique being. Of course, the infant has no clue as to where to start or what exactly it is looking for. It wanders about then returns unfulfilled to mother, only to try to break away again. Frustration, fear, despair, and bewilderment rush through the poor child. The entire gamut of human emotions is experienced by the unprepared psyche.

Because the Modern Separation process is filled with such tremendous emotional conflict the coinciding experience of the infant's working to define itself, working to create an acceptable ego, is equally difficult. In the Modern Individuation process a young child trying to learn who and what it is encounters the world around it with trepidation and anxiety. It sees and hears and touches the physical reality around it. But all of these sensations are filled with questions. The child has not been given the opportunity to observe how other human beings interact with the same environment. The infant experiences the world with a need to find food and shelter and avoid dangers. It has not had the time to learn the wisdom of all who came before. By separating themselves from their mothers and the secure guidance their mothers can provide, Modern infants are only afforded solo trial-and-error assessment of their environments. They are plagued by urgency. They do not know when mother will actually finally abandon them. They must learn to survive. They fight everyone and everything out of frustration. They defend their egos. It is a difficult way to learn how and where they fit into the grand scheme of things. Individuation, the path to the Modern understanding of self, suffers from not having enough time to complete a satisfactory education. Even after thousands of centuries of species survival every new Modern human baby starts from zero, on its own.

Constancy
"Peek-a-boo, I see you!"
We play with the new baby. We stare at it and smile. Then we put our hands in front of our faces. We wait for a second or two, then we pull our hands aside and smile at the little one. The baby often looks momentarily shocked then laughs to see the familiar faces smiling. It is a simple game that has been perpetuated for millennia. It is the early reinforcing of a fundamental intellectual and psychological development that every newborn must acquire to survive.

Psychologists name it object-constancy or object-permanence. They talk about "internalizing". Simply put, it is the knowledge that an object or, more importantly, a person, still exists when it is not being physically experienced by one or more of the five senses. It is the knowledge that eventually gives us the understanding that even though the sun goes down beyond the western horizon it will be back again in the morning. It is the knowledge that when we turn away from looking at a tree it is yet a tree planted where we saw it. The tree did not relocate its position, and it did not change to something else. Object-constancy gives us the understanding that when we walk past a rock it will not suddenly become a lion or a rabbit. It will always be a rock. Emotional object-constancy is required to establish a psychologically healthy mother-child relationship. The knowledge that mother can be counted on, that she will still be there, and that she will always love her child is necessary for that individual to progress through the Separation-Individuation process.

Acquiring an inner sense of constancy naturally begins with an infant's relationship with its mother. Its mother is the source of the child's first sensory perceptions. For the first six months mother is 90% of an infant's awareness. If mother is constant the world is consistent. The psyche will have a firm foundation upon which to grow. If mother is inconsistent the perceived world is unpredictable. The psyche will only be able to build on shifting sands.

We have discussed the profound effects nomadic and permanent residence lifestyles had on the Separation-Individuation process. A nomad mother's presence was absolute. She was a continual physical presence for three, four, or even five years. Because sedentary lifestyles allowed a mother to set her baby down in a secure place mother world was not the same physical presence. A baby had doubt of mother's commitment to the baby's well-being almost as soon as awareness of mother began. For 150,000 years children grew up without doubt about mother and therefore without doubt about the world or life. Ten thousand years ago doubt opened the door for imaginary creatures, irrational fears, and Supernatural beings.

Delving into the concept of object-constancy leads to other insights. The baby of early prehistoric times living within a small nomadic society had the obvious constancy of mother from the very first. Care-provider, nurturer, and transport vehicle, mother provided for all of baby's needs without prompting. With an infant's growing awareness the human beings who were present every day became other intimate constants. The extended family of individuals living interdependently for survival were always a part of the infant's growing sensory awareness. The voices, smells, facial traits, and physical mannerisms imprinted themselves in the baby's mind. Natural environments could change every day if the group was searching for food or water. The environment was not the stable foundation of daily reality. The human family, the tight-knit social band, was the constant daily reality.

In later times when children were born in fixed dwellings, the newborn was surrounded by fixed physical objects whose sights, smells, and textures never changed. Never changing is the very definition of constancy. The relationship of object-constancy with mother, however, had its difficulties. Babies no longer needed to be held safe from a potentially hostile environment or carried for long treks. A mother could put her baby down in a safe place and leave for minutes at a time. She would disappear from the sight and hearing of her infant. She came and went. An infant lost the presence of the only security it knew. Constancy of care and nourishment was a very big question mark for the child new to this world. All living things came and went. Domesticated farm animals, dogs, cats, mice, rats, insects, and human beings all passed through baby's sensory perception. Other human beings were not the foundation of constancy upon which baby's growing intelligence was built. It was stationary inanimate things that baby first defined as "real".

Sibling Rivalry

The phenomenon psychologists define as sibling rivalry is a recent development. It had not existed before ten thousand years ago. The homo sapiens species for its entire previous existence had not had to deal with the trauma of sibling rivalry. No human infant had ever suffered or endured its heartache and distress.

When a mother must take care of two or three children who have not matured beyond the formative Separation-Individuation process those children are caught in the worst possible turmoil. Sibling rivalry is about the most fundamental life-and-death competition. The fear of losing mother's sustaining closeness quickly leads to competition for mother's love.

Siblings vying for attention, nutrition, and protection create a circumstance of accelerating emotional and psychological tension. They are in a battle of wits with their siblings. It is not a fight they have been prepared for. They will modify their behavior until they achieve the best results they can manage. They will do this by trial and error which is the only choice they have been given. They are too young to define the situation verbally. They will cry, cry louder, modulate their screams, or be silent. They will wriggle, kick, pinch, cuddle, or go limp. They will continue whichever actions yield the best results until these actions no longer work to attract attention. Then they will readjust their behavior. During this entire process they are motivated by fear of losing mother's life-giving companionship. They blame their siblings, and they blame their mothers. They are jealous of the attention paid to someone else. At times they feel helpless.

As the infant endures the situation, it understands that it must become responsible for its own survival. Mother is not reliable. There are forces working to distract mother from her duty to the infant. Mostly these forces are another sibling. As the child begins to acquire mobility it is also acquiring the method by which it may be able to learn to fend for itself. So begins the Separation process. It is always a period of emotional ups and downs. Little victories of being able to venture into the world and experience physical reality through the senses bring elation and confidence. Small setbacks of failures to accomplish activities that underdeveloped muscles will not yet allow are accompanied by depression and anger. The need to still depend on mother through the three years of this psychological growth creates impatience and a lack of confidence. The self image attempting to be created is caught in a seesaw of positive and negative. With every failure is the understanding that this situation would have been different and perhaps unnecessary if the other sibling had not interfered. All of this occurs as the child is learning about the world, about living in human society, and trying to grow physically, mentally, and emotionally. The foundation of its life is being set. Everything else in life will be built upon this awkward foundation. It is a wonder any sane human being can emerge.

The emotion of jealousy, the assigning of blame, and the need to compete against a sibling for mother's attention and care are the wellspring of distrust, of greed, and of violent aggressive behavior. An individual feels no agreeable bond with its brother or sister. The bond with its mother, tainted by feelings of resentment and abandonment, is ambiguous at best.

Sibling rivalry not only undermines the mother-child relationship it destabilizes any relationships with other persons. Doubt, fear, and suspicion will color every human interaction. The individual certainly does not look favorably on strangers. Cooperation with others is replaced by competition. Individual and social group behaviors are never sure. Emotional experiences are heightened. Brain mechanisms of problem solving and perception always contain an element of uncertainty. Self preservation is ultimate. He or she is alone in this world and chooses to make social ties and friendships only as they can benefit himself or herself.

Ten thousand years ago sibling rivalry, such a small little thing, opened a Pandora's box of human insecurity that, once opened, was never able to contain again the plagues of fear and resentment and inadequacy that fill Modern psyches.

Archaic versus Modern

Contrary to what many would like to believe, human nature is not inherent biology.

Human nature is an acquired psychology.

Simple hunter-gatherers are the obvious proof. They are the same biological homo sapiens as we are. But their human nature is not our human nature.

There is strong evidence that our semi-nomadic hunter-gatherer ancestors possessed a psychological profile such as the world discovered in the natural, unspoiled cultures of the Polar Eskimos and the Kalahari Ju/wasi. These peoples were socially nonaggressive and nonviolent. They lived closely and openly with each other without quarrel, resentment, or condescension. They displayed no signs of egotism or self-consciousness. They were confident without pride. They were independent. They showed respect and appreciation for others. They did so without ego driven emotions, without feelings of inferiority or feelings of superiority. They were noncompetitive in every aspect of social behavior. This is not a description that fits any modern or historic civilized peoples.

The psychological development of human beings who inhabited this Earth prior to 10,000 years ago was different from the psychological development which we experience today. This one plain fact so easily and so astutely explains so much.

The psychological shift ultimately became the personality shift evidenced in early prehistoric hunter-gatherer and Modern Civilized man. Given our understanding of infant psychological development, simple hunter-gatherers did actually have different personalities. It is not that they were simply well-mannered. They understood the world differently. We understand all social behaviors in terms of do's and don'ts. These people had no such concept. We base many actions on often unreasonable fears. They had no irrational fears. We are combative and self-oriented. They were collaborative and selfless.

The Separation-Individuation Process, the weaning of an infant from its mother's care and the defining of its self, had not existed more than 10,000 years ago. If we accept that the ego was greatly minimized in Eskimo and Ju/wa societies, the stage of psychological development that we recognize as Separation-Individuation would have merely been a process of slow awareness without the anxiety and trauma of lost security and nurture, without the need to assuage a premature ego.

An individual raised through the Archaic psychological process neither separated from its mother nor identified itself as an individual. It always remained close to its mother into adulthood and remained an integral part of the same small group of people it continued to live with throughout its life. Because there were no close siblings the child never had a need to bolster a self-image in order to compete for mother's attention. This child with a completely fulfilled psyche established secure relationships with everyone and everything in its life. It was always an accepted part of a connected, mutually supporting community. The process was not Separation-Individuation. It was Secure Identity.

This psychological character allowed sharing amongst a group to be conducted without jealousy or selfishness. No one placed his or her needs above those of the others. No one desired to have more than another. This seemingly selfless generosity and this humble nature were not quite what we understand today. Our thinking is ego-centric. Human beings living 20,000 years ago were entirely without self. As there was no selfish behavior, there was no un-selfish behavior.

Sibling rivalry has affected startling changes in human behavior. Its effects are not limited to the immediate children who had competing brothers and sisters. A child does not need to actually have a sibling present during its S-I process to be affected by the sibling rivalry phenomenon. Once competition and selfish, anti-social behaviors began, they spread throughout the global population. Sibling rivalry tore every social fabric apart. The careful, controlled weaving of interpersonal respect and consideration that had existed for 150,000 years became unraveled when antagonism, personal animosities, and selfish behaviors could no longer be tempered with civility. After several hundred years, after 10 or 15 generations, the metamorphosis was so complete within human society that no one could remember anything different.

Chapter notes

1. Margaret S. Mahler and Fred Pine and Anni Bergman, The Psychological Development of the Human Infant, [????:
Basic Books, 1975], 3
2. R. Buckminster Fuller, YouTube website:http://www.youtube.com/watch?v=o6yaSLipeWg uploaded May 26, 2011
3. Lorna J. Marshall, The !Kung of the Nyae Nyae, [Cambridge, Massachusetts: Harvard,1976], 315
4. Mahler, Human Infant, 59

6. Corollaries to the Psychological Shift

Art

Having given consideration to the change in the normal psychological development of human infants we can revisit some of the earlier observations regarding prehistoric mankind. The lack of human beings in the cave art of Ice Age southwestern Europe seems to have an obvious rationale. The dramatic switch to narrative paintings inhabited by a plethora of human figures running and dancing also seems to have a good explanation. Very simply put, human beings before the Seed of Civilization did not have a psychological affinity for self-centered thought, either individually or as a species. They were seemingly oblivious, totally without self-awareness. The more proper understanding is that they gave themselves no special importance. People were the normal, common everyday reality. Human beings who lived after the Seed of Civilization was sown were completely self-absorbed as individuals and therefore as a species. Everything they did was important and interesting.

Sharing

Understanding an infant's development of constancy gives us another clue into the behavioral habit of sharing as part of early prehistoric groups. Sharing meat was integral to nomadic societies. The practice of giving and receiving food equally somehow was lost in later agricultural societies where hierarchies of merit and entitlement replaced the democratic allotment of food.

Sharing was fundamental for early homo sapiens. The family of persons who traveled together day after day, who worked efficiently in a coordinated partnership, who were the music and the dance and the bouquet of a growing infant's psyche, established all of the sensory and cognitive roots upon which a new human being would base its awareness of the world. This small social and economic band of human beings was the conduit that moved the child through the ever-challenging puzzle of reality. The practice of sharing sustenance with each other was not simply a practical strategy for biological survival. Giving support to each other, respecting each other, and being completely open with each other continually reaffirmed the intellectual and emotional definitions of what life was. Reality as each one of these people knew it had been founded on the object-constancy of the others in the small community. The knowledge that there was a physical world that would not change had had its primal psychological origin in mother and this extended family. Sharing, ultimately, was a reinforcing of one's world. Sharing not only supported the community with physical nutrition, but it also nurtured the psychological being of each individual. It supported the very fabric of human relations that every individual's object-constancy had been built upon. Sharing was, in truth, a way for the individual to reinforce its own psychological foundation. Sharing strengthened the small community of people who had given each child's developing psyche a rock upon which to build emotional stability. Sharing was reassuring and comforting for each person, and it was a subtle thank-you to all others.

"There is no privacy in [Ju/wa] lifestyle. They live in each other's presence without walls. They build little grass shelters but live outside them by a fire. The family fires are clustered only a few feet apart so their combined light at night holds out the darkness and the prowling beasts. Being near together, able to see and touch each other, is security and comfort to the [Ju/wasi]." [1]

Scholars have looked at the strict sharing traditions among the Polar Eskimos and the Kalahari Ju/wasi as a means of keeping egos in check, keeping any single member of the group from being held in higher esteem than others, and keeping individuals from thinking of themselves as contributing more than others. But with the understanding that closeness to others within the small community was wished for by all, perhaps the acts of sharing were meant to keep any member from feeling inferior. Psychologically, each individual depended on the whole group. Stress within a group was paramount to trauma for each individual. Keeping everyone in the band secure and content bolstered each individual's support group.

Sociologists and anthropologists often cite peer pressure as a form of regulation among close-knit groups. A group controls misbehavior and disobedience by threats of ostracizing, shunning, or ignoring any individual who steps out of line. This may be true for Modern agricultural societies and even for complex hunter-gatherer societies. But with the knowledge we have acquired regarding simple hunter-gatherers (and therefore all of our early prehistoric ancestors) it is more reasonable to think of a peer bond rather than peer pressure in these societies. Peer pressure is about obeying rules. It is a form of negative reinforcement. Simple hunter-gatherers lived without rules. Their social choices were something deeper and more compelling. A peer bond is a positive supporting of the group by each individual. Among hunter-gatherers no individual wanted to disturb or disrupt his or her family of friends. Consideration for all was the underlying motivation for these people.

Anthropocentrism

Why did the world become anthropocentric?
Because human beings became ego-centric.

From the beginning and for 150,000 years human egos were almost non-existent. Then an unplanned change subtly altered the relationship of mother and child. It effected the psychological development of every infant, and it spread throughout the growing population of human beings.

When each human infant felt abandoned by its mother it needed ego, self identity, and self-assurance. Humanity took on the same psychological needs that each individual person had. The "self" identity of humanity needed to be defined. Humanity needed to build a collective self-esteem. It needed to be better than other beings. Humanity now functioned better if it could place itself above animals and Nature. Human beings were the epitome of living things. Indeed, they were separate from all other living things. Human beings had souls. God had placed men as stewards over the earth and all therein. In bolstering their collective egos some communities placed themselves above other groups of "inferior" people. They became the True People or the Chosen Ones. Others became Infidels and Aliens. As individuals found acclaim in competitions, so did groups and societies seek fame. In the same way that individuals wanted possessions to set themselves apart from other people, so did cities, nations, and religions collect wealth. All of these high goals and glory and magnificence were beyond the realm of other living things. Men focused on the activities of men. They were much more interesting and of more clever designs than the quiet natural world.

A culture of self-focused individuals had no room for lesser things. Modern history has been about aggrandizing human egos. Both individual and collective egos have driven invention, exploration, war, and conquest. Anthropocentric ego has left the planet and its natural resources ravaged. Mankind has given no concern for other species or natural waters or its mountains of industrial waste. Most of the damage has been unintentional, simply thoughtless. Because anthropocentrism and the egos that shape it are oblivious to anything but human desire and whim.

Alcohol

Agriculture fostered another change in human beings that was equally as devastating as the increase in birthrate. It was the advent of agriculture that gave rise to the routine consumption of alcohol. When we consider how important the early psychological growth of human infants is to individuals and society as a whole, alcohol could have played a very relevant role in altering the rational thought processes of prehistoric men.

Early agricultural communities found that without a means of preservation the abundance of a harvest would inevitably rot. Beverages such as beer, mead, and wine which were made from grains, vegetables, honey, and fruits provided a solution to the problem. Allowing harvested crops to ferment enabled farmers to keep the nutritional value of the foods through periods of winter or drought. The process of fermentation resulted in the production of alcoholic liquids which human beings found consumable and perhaps enjoyable.

Unfortunately, alcohol is a drug to the human metabolism and will have an effect on human behavior. Over-indulging in alcohol can do strange things to the behavior of anyone drinking it. It changes the body's blood chemistry and effects the brain's ability to react in acceptable ways. Reaction time is slowed. Good judgement is hampered. Muscle coordination can be lost.

The most devastating effect of alcohol is not on those who partake and then temporarily lose their balance and their inhibitions. It is on the infants and children who begin their lives in the surroundings of those under the influence. A good insight into the extended effects of alcohol abuse in a family or communal situation can be learned from the Adult Children of Alcoholics support group.

Adult children of alcoholics may not necessarily be alcoholics themselves. In many cases they have seen the damage alcoholism can do to their parents and have avoided drinking alcohol completely. But their parents' alcoholism has effected the very core of their psyches and their abilities to understand life and define reality.

A typical sentiment heard over and over would be, "I was never sure who would come home... my caring, happy-go-lucky father or a loud abusive monster who looked like him."

All children learn to live life by observing the world around them. From the time of their births, infants' observations of parents, siblings, and immediate society shape their behavior, their social consciousness, and developing psyches. From earliest infancy children learn acceptable emotions and actions through the behavioral feedback of others.

It is easy to see how the use of alcohol by people within the sphere of an infant's developmental years effects that child throughout its entire life. People who drink alcohol do not behave in the same manner when sober as when they are drinking. They exhibit obvious changes in their interaction with others. Their physical mannerisms change. Their speech will slur. They can overreact. They can be slow to respond. They can stumble and bump into things or people. For a young child observing this it is very confusing. The child can observe no behavioral constants. The child's actions that elicited favorable responses from a sober parent now induce ridiculing laughter or rage or indifference.

Since the advent of agriculture children of alcoholics were never allowed to observe valid patterns of social behavior in their parents. Under the influence of alcohol their mothers and/or their fathers had inconsistent, multiple, often volatile personalities, and it was almost impossible to predict when or how which character would appear. A child could not develop behavior patterns that would consistently achieve proper reaction from alcoholic parents.

As a stone tossed into a pond creates concentric ripples through water, so does the use of alcohol which chemically alters personal behaviors create psychological effects through generations of family and society. The young developing children of alcoholics, always struggling to understand the patterns of the world around them, will grow up to be adult children of alcoholics. And they will have children of their own who will learn from the language and actions of their parents that a dependable reality upon which to base their lives does not exist. And these lost children when adults will have children of their own.

It is well within the realm of possibility that alcohol had a more direct effect on young children. If a nursing mother ingested alcohol, the alcohol would affect her breastmilk. Her infant would unwittingly be subjected to the chemical effects. It is also possible that children could have been fed alcoholic beverages for sustenance. Even if rationed and limited to avoid inebriation, alcohol would affect the body chemistry of the young more readily than that of adults. This practice need not have continued over a long period. If merely for one or two generations the collective effect on the fabric of the human psyche would have been irreparable. It may have been a question of either fermented drink or starvation, there being no choice but to feed children with the available nourishment. Still, the slightest altering of mental or emotional abilities during the critical and sensitive period of Separation-Individuation would have been devastating.

The comments about alcohol must include the fact that neither the Greenland Eskimos nor the Ju/wa bushmen drank alcohol or were even aware of alcohol as a consumable beverage. Alcohol had no influence on the lives of these people as individuals or as a community.

Chapter notes

1. Lorna J. Marshall, Nyae Nyae !Kung Beliefs and RItes, [Cambridge, Massachusetts: Harvard, 1999], 59

Part II. The Creation of Civilization

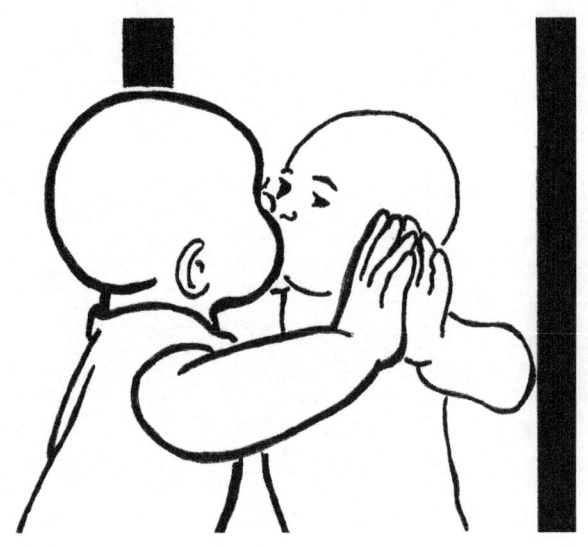

7. Ego, the Seed of Civilization

The Seed of Civilization was sown in the minds of men. It germinated and grew. It was a little nothing, but it was fertile. Once it began to take root nothing could contain it. It was aggressive, and when aggressive meets non-aggressive the non-aggressive yields or succumbs. The Seed of Civilization spread like wildfire.

The Seed of Civilization, that minuscule mote, was the needy, desperate ego of every infant who experienced the Modern Separation-Individuation process. It was a psychological aberration new to the homo sapiens species. It thrived on competition. It was suspicious. It masked itself from others. It twitched with paranoia. It desired attention.

Such a thing cannot exist freely in a human society. It is destructive to social bonds and friendships. It creates antagonism towards every other human being. It has doubt about every natural reality. It is unsure of itself. It is self-destructive. Such a thing cannot survive in a species. The species will disintegrate and disappear from the evolutionary chain.

Yet for ten thousand years homo sapiens have prolonged the inevitable. The human brain has performed miracle after miracle to keep our species alive. Verbal abstraction, the Supernatural, hierarchical strata, and disciplinary rules were born from the mind's thin air, fleshed out, and refined. They were all part of a survival mechanism. It was psychological survival not biological survival. Surprisingly, with the receding of the Last Ice Age and with the advent of agriculture biological survival had never been easier.

The raison d'être for all of Civilization was the premature, unfulfilled human ego. Civilization was born from the need to support the anomaly of the human ego. Civilization became the means by which each individual could support its ego in the context of a social group. Civilization was the structure that fostered definition and order to every modern psyche. Without such order every new, struggling psyche would be lost forever in a world of perceived chaos.

Competition for mother's attention and a search for consistencies in the physical world and in social interactions motivate every Modern young child and subconsciously motivate every Modern adult. Such was not the case in early prehistoric times. But sibling rivalry and an absent mother changed all of that. Competition and a search for constancy have driven history.

Sibling rivalry encourages aggressive competition towards others. An immature ego wants to attract attention and recognition. This behavior begins with an infant's urgency for its mother, but it becomes a foundation for all social interactions. Dominating and coercing others is a manifestation of this. It is an attempt to boost one's ego by feeling superior to others. In essence it is showing mother why she should choose you first. Needing to be better than others manifests itself physically and symbolically. Every athletic victory, every accumulation of wealth, and every display of status are reassurances of superiority. Any behavior that draws attention to oneself, that makes one stand out in a crowd is similarly ego based. It is the primal psyche trying to impress mother.

We can all understand such behavior in terms of individuals and people we know. It is when we begin to extrapolate personal behaviors into an understanding of our cultures and our species that we see origins of Civilization. It is critical to remember that simple hunter-gatherers lived differently. Aggression and violence are not inherent in the human species. Competition and domination are not biologically part of our undeniable nature. Our species should not be compared to wolves and lions. We may be more like elephants and whales. Simple hunter-gatherers are the proper model for the homo sapiens species. But mankind altered the archetype.

How much of history is about coercion and dominating others? Every war and every campaign of conquest is exactly that. Wars have been fought at the drop of a hat because of an insult, because of culturally biased hatred, or because someone simply wanted to control bigger populations and their riches. Historically, governments have operated through many types of coercive control. Enslavement, debilitating taxation, censorship, and intimidation have all been part of government policies. Religious institutions and social class systems function by authoritarian control. Converting others to one's intellectual beliefs and demanding sworn allegiance are dominating behaviors. Financial coercion is equally tyrannical. Attempts to bankrupt others or gain monopolies are fiscal bullying.

There is no biological or evolutionary reason for such behavior.

How much of culture is directly related to self-aggrandizing and calling attention to oneself? Elite status in academic achievement, in athletic achievement, and in business are about being better than others. The desire for status exudes in the nuance and brashness of daily life: cars, neighborhoods, job titles, marriage partners, social cliques, jewelry, and designer fashions. Standing out in a crowd is the very definition of fashion. Fashion in it's zillions of facets: clothing, hairstyles, jewelry, and make-up, is the ultimate in egocentric ritual.
None of these behaviors has precedence in early prehistoric societies.

A young infant's psychological search for consistency is a search for definition. To make one's way through life there must be finite realities from which to evaluate situations when solving problems and making choices. Ever-present doubt during the Modern S-I process short-circuits any intellectual or emotional constancy. Doubt can never really be overcome. It is a fear that must be faced continuously throughout life.
Many components of Civilization were created simply to put off and allay doubt. They were prefabricated definitions for life. Community rules and regulations were codified. Ethical and moral etiquettes were established. Rituals were choreographed and given symbolic significance. Ideologies were given denotation and connotation.
Each of these social accoutrements gave the Modern S-I psyche firm patterns to grasp. When young minds could not observe consistent social patterns then verbal teaching allowed those minds to superimpose an already accepted standard. Doubt about proper or correct social behaviors was eliminated simply by adhering to the established guidelines.
Consider these words that Civilization has given us:
True and false; win and lose; Good and Evil.
None of these abstract concepts existed in simple hunter-gatherer societies. Such ideas had nothing to do with daily living.
All of the six concepts were established to help Modern individuals define life and social relationships. Without such verbal abstractions there would simply have been chaos. So language was used to define patterns via symbolic representation. This has been true for the past ten thousand years.

True and false were defined by Civilization because individuals acquired different opinions about what was real. What is real in the physical world should be obvious to all. But when doubt about constancy was introduced to the human psyche realness was lost. Only individual opinions were created. By consensus societies established verities. True and false were born. Yet even today different cultures around the world hold different opinions about what is true and what is false. Even absolutes are subjective.

Win and lose are the end result of competition. In simple hunter-gatherer societies there was no competition. They had no competitive games or social status. Competition was a dramatic evocation by sibling rivalry. Competition is evaluating oneself against others. Surprisingly, being better than another was not satisfying enough for the Modern ego. Being better had to be conclusive. Win and lose became the absolutes of competition. When win and lose could not satisfy greedy egos then more abstract verbalizations of success and failure were created.

Right and wrong were defined by Civilization because individuals grew up with their own observations about how people interacted. There was not the consistency of social interactions that there had been among our egalitarian, selfless ancestors. Society needed to establish acceptable behaviors for all to learn and follow. Concepts of right and wrong were later taken out of the realm of simple social interactions and were elevated to further abstraction of motive. Good and Evil were born. In a society of self-interested persons simply defining right and wrong or Good and Evil were not sufficient to ensure correct behaviors. Rules and regulation were needed. Crime and punishment were established. Heaven and Hell were born.

Understanding the differences between our early prehistoric ancestors and Modern man reveals how much the new psyche has affected Civilization. Power, wealth, and fame drive our cultures and all those within. Power speaks of grandeur and control. Our forebears were egalitarian. Power had no sense. Wealth is an accumulation of economic possessions. Our forebears had no sense of possession. They had no sense of mine versus yours. Wealth was without meaning. Fame is the ultimate self-centeredness. Our forebears avoided the least attention to themselves. Fame would have been anathema.

What changed about human societies and human beings?

Socially, for 150,000 years:
    They lived without rules of ethical behavior.
    They lived without leaders or elders or shamans.
    They lived without religion.
    They lived without marriage.
Behaviorally, for 150,000 years:
    They lived without status. They were egalitarian.
    They lived without competition.
    They lived without fear.
Intellectually, for 150,000 years:
    They lived without philosophy.
    They lived without defining right and wrong.
    They lived without history.

Then came a 99% flip.

For all of recorded history we have had rules, political leaders, religion, and possessions. For all of recorded history we have been class conscious, competitive, and fearful.

For all of recorded history we have tried to define the meaning of life, debated good and evil, and sought to record human achievement.

How did that happen? It was most certainly the psychological alteration to human development that was at the root of this transformation. The advent of agriculture is often touted as the root cause for Civilization. Agriculture did not inspire war or thievery. Greed is not fostered by a bounty of food and resources. It should be the opposite. With plenty there is no need to worry about one's survival. There should be no violence or argument with one's neighbors. Life is easy. What is there to complain about?

Having come to the realization that Civilization in its many aspects only came into existence after the psychological shift, it remains to demonstrate how the Seed of Civilization took root and grew. The growth of Civilization was not by chance. It was shaped with the care and craft of a potted bonsai. Isolated from Nature it was bound and contorted to the needs of the human psyche. Every aspect of our Modern culture was cultivated by egos with specific purpose.

The whole phenomenon of Civilization was a rapid evolution. It grew out of a desperate necessity to calm and coddle premature egos. There was logical sequence, and there was rationale for every transformation. The sowing of Civilization had definable aspects that reveal how and why it came to be.

8. Doubt and Loss

For 150,000 years there was no inkling of Civilization, not the slightest whisper of the amazing things humanity would yet bequeath to this earth. It was not that hunter-gatherers were not clever enough to create elaborate bureaucracies, stylish glamour, and lavish wealth. Simple hunter-gatherers had no need of such things. Nor did they desire things beyond that which was necessary for survival. Their fully realized psyches needed no pampering or buttressing, no boost or acclaim. They enjoyed life and the people with whom they shared it.

Doubt, loss of confidence, emotional loss, and irrational fears haunted the human beings who created Civilization. They continue to hound us today. These angsts are the legacy of the Modern Separation-Individuation process fostered by sibling rivalry and a disengaged mother. We are not just talking about little doubts that one might have passing through the day. We are talking about deep-rooted doubts: philosophical, religious, moral, and psychological doubts. We assume them to be part of the human condition. But they are not.

Simple hunter-gatherers had no doubts. They had no moral rules, no religious beliefs or rituals, and no philosophical thinking. They lived life assuredly because they knew nothing else. From infancy all individuals acquired the skills to find food, make tools and fire, and traverse immense landscapes. They were intimately aware of the natural world. They knew every living thing, where and how it grew, and what it could be used for. They knew the signs and cycles of weather. All of these things are foregone conclusions; without such knowledge our ancestors would not have survived. They lived with the confidence of a prize fighter who has never lost a bout or a marathon runner who has never lost a race.

Hunter-gatherers had no fears of the unknown because everything in their world was known. Before the advent of the Modern ego the world was a definable reality. It was finite not infinite. The natural world was observed with five senses and understood by its unchanging patterns.

Hunter-gatherers knew only one way to live: do what was necessary and face what life brought without fear or complaint. That is not to say that these men and women had no fear when facing a lion or bear or charging bison. The point is that the fear was not irrational. They faced aggressive predators, and with determination and skill they would often prevail. It will ever be a guess as to what kind of ego and personality a complete and fully realized Archaic Secure Identity development can yield. But that is what human beings had until ten thousand years ago. There is evidence in the Kalahari Ju/wasi and in the Greenland Polar Eskimos. Individuals were independent and capable. Each shared with others, but no one felt they were owed in return.

The revelations regarding the Archaic Secure Identity process give a plausible rationale for superlatively capable human beings. Life was learned at a mother's breast. A child whose psychological development was nurtured with care and full attention from its mother would have had the optimum chance to avoid psychological trauma and neuroses. It would have been happy. It would have had a completely satisfied psychological maturation.

A maturely developed ego was confident without pride. It was imperturbable. It would have had no need to do irrational or selfish things to call attention to itself or bolster its self-image.

Lonely? Confused? Angry? Depressed? These very human feelings have only existed for ten thousand years.

The advent of human psyches that were denied complete maturation changed the human species. Psyches were traumatized forever after. People lost the self-assurance that had characterized their ancestors for thousands of years. They suffered from emotional loss. They became prey to doubts and fears.

Doubt caused by the inability to establish consistent and constant patterns was perhaps the worst. It was an intellectual doubt about the world in which one lived. There was no connection with nature. Individuals became ineffectual when dealing with the physical world. Physical reality was questionable. Physical laws were not assured. The brain became handicapped. With doubts the mind could not function at peak efficiency. Doubt was the ultimate cause of irrational fears and loss of confidence. Doubt plagued the ego's constant search for self-value. Doubt led to social mistrust and social misunderstandings. Human beings were beset by worry and a constant nagging to answer "Why?".

Fear was no longer a biological impetus to boost reaction time and mental focus. Fear now originated in the realm of the imagination. It was fear of the unknown. It was fear of incredible possibilities without any foundation for such fear. Fear became foolish, preposterous, and rampant. It resulted in inappropriate responses and inaction. It caused an avoidance of social interactions. It caused intolerance and nonacceptance of others.

Fear and doubt eroded the confidence that had characterized simple hunter-gatherer individuals. Persons who lacked confidence overcompensated. They became aggressive and egotistic to hide their insecurity, or they became dependent and relied on others. Lacking absolute confidence they hesitated. They acted without assurance. They second guessed. They were never sure of any action or emotion or thought.

The psychological trauma of mother's perceived abandonment by every young infant completely altered human emotions and social contacts. It did so on such a profoundly subconscious and pre-verbal level as to be hidden from our awareness and thinking for hundreds of generations until Freud delved into humanity's collective psyche. Emotional loss enshrouded individuals with sadness and insecurity. In turn they reacted with secrecy, fears of commitment, and domination of others. They needed constant assurance and became possessive, not as in a desire for physical things but as in a need for unfailing attention from another. Emotional loss affected interpersonal relationships, especially the most intimate. Individuals sought to regain the close bonds they had had with their mothers in their earliest infancies. Intellectually they acquired a need to seek fulfillment and a meaning to life.

Fear and doubt are debilitating. They fill a person with confusion, suspicion, indecision, and misgivings. They fill society with the same. An individual's whole being and perception of life is ambivalent and uncertain. Society is ambivalent and uncertain. The foundation of all things is unstable and shaky.

How can anyone survive when faced with perpetual doubt? A life filled with doubt is a life filled with unfounded fears. One is constantly reassessing one's decisions and motives. One has no idea what the physical world is capable of. Procrastination becomes pandemic. Biological survival cannot withstand instability and uncertainty.

Suffering psychological deprivation the minds of infants born to Modern parents have never been given the opportunity to fully realize the patterns of life. Ever since the emergence of the Modern S-I process the minds of newborns have never been able to function properly. They have never been able to see valid social patterns in their environment. That uncertainty has also influenced perception of the natural world.

The perception that mother was unreliable understandably frightened an infant. It felt that it must fend for itself without assistance from anyone or anything. The world was chaotic. The only verifiable reality was its own existence. Each tiny baby became the center of its very own universe.

There was now an intellectual and psychological necessity for immature and traumatized psyches to define themselves and discover the means of surviving. Everything was perceived through the prism of ego. The universe was evaluated subjectively with a self-centered bias. Object constancy failed to reach maturity in ego-centric psyches. Patterns were no longer observed coolly and rationally. Intellectually, the infinite weaving of life had become merely loose threads.

Chaos was perceived by every child, and every child beheld a different chaos, his or her own individually perceived chaos. There was chaos in the physical world, and there was chaos in the social relationships between people. Viewing the world as fraught with chaos was the natural outcome of a life filled with doubt and loss. There was no respite. There was no direction. There was no reason.

When the world is utter chaos how can one proceed?
Humanity had come to an impasse.

Ten thousand years ago humanity faced extinction because of a psychological shift. Yet as a species we are still thriving. Of dire necessity the human brain somehow twisted and jury-rigged a scheme for human society and each individual to survive. That scheme became Civilization.

With persuasion and coercion Civilization became the strategy for overcoming humanity's newly acquired affliction.

Marriage

Marriage is a perfect example of how Civilization grew within human societies to calm and quell the deep anxieties festering in Modern minds.

In Modern societies the ultimate expression of an intimate relationship and bond between a man and a woman is marriage. The institution of marriage is so prevalent that it has been considered a natural part to every human society since the beginning of our species. Yet for 150,000 years human beings lived without marriage. Simple hunter-gatherers did not marry. A man and a woman paired, often for their lifetimes, but they did this without vows or ceremonies or celebrations. It was a pragmatic union making their lives easier. The commitment each had to the other was respect and understanding. There were no rules or laws. There was no talk of eternal love.

Marriage today, however, is all about rules and laws. It is about solemn vows and obedience. It is sworn commitment backed by social pressures and governmental laws. It is in the sight of God and forever, until death. How and why did a simple, respectful relationship become knotted and entangled by binding dogma?

Marriage is about two human beings in the most profound of interpersonal relationships. Ever since the Modern S-I process began 10,000 years ago doubt and fear have affected every social and interpersonal relationship. Yielding to the most intimate of relationships has always been biologically and emotionally and psychologically fulfilling. It has also become psychologically terrifying. That is because anyone's first intimate relationship is the mother-child bond experienced during infancy. The lesson learned by every Modern infant is that mother is inconsistent and ultimately unreliable. Love disintegrates. The lesson teaches sadness and abandonment. Yet we all hunger for that first emotional closeness which once existed with the original "Love Object".

Psychologists sometimes refer to an infant's mother as "the Love Object". The term Love Object refers to any person (not really an object) with whom the individual has a deep, intimate relationship. The concept behind this somewhat awkward designation relates to any and all intimate relationships throughout a person's life. Not surprisingly those love relationships have a deep-rooted psychological link with the first intimate relationship an infant had with its mother. Because the Modern S-I process is experienced by an infant as an unwanted separation from mother's care that sense of loss will shadow all future love relationships. Irrational possessiveness, anger when wishes are not fulfilled, and fear of abandonment are all symptoms of love relationships that stem from infantile feelings of perceived rejection by mother. We long to mend that broken bond. We believe it is possible to find original happiness again. But we are hesitant and afraid. We dream fantasies, and we demand fulfillment. We alter our personalities and judgements. It is an emotional roller coaster.

Civilization long ago worked to create a necessary support for our fragile egos and our haunting doubts. It set about to guarantee happiness in marriage. It defined structure and delineated bounds. Official papers must now be signed and recorded. Promises must be made. Never again would we lose that one and only someone who would love and care for us unconditionally. Civilization declared the marriage relationship to be unbreakable and legally binding. So much so that even when a relationship deteriorates or evolves it cannot be easily dissolved. The husband and wife are treated as the physical property of each other. (Though this is often weighed in favor of the husband since male domination has come to define Modern societies.) Civilization's social and religious institutions hold strict regulations for the marriage union. Forgiveness of unacceptable behaviors in the marriage is often more important than respect and honesty. Civilization does all that it can to maintain the declared bond of intimacy.

Civilization created background support for marriage with fairy tales of princesses and princes, dreams of lost-and-found Soulmates, ideals of the One-in-the-World-for-Me, and the state of Eternal Bliss. They are transparent attempts to recreate the lost emotional and psychological bond of mother's love. Philosophy and literature examine the search for cosmic wholeness and for the completion of self in loving and being loved by another. Through popular songs, magazine ads, movies, and a whole genre of best-selling novels the propaganda of True Romance is preached and advertised perpetually and ubiquitously.

Civilization accompanies the social mythology of marital bliss with lavish celebrations and costume. The wedding is a bride's happiest day, the moment she looks forward to all her life as a girl and young woman. It is the culmination of her life's dream. Small fortunes are paid as dowery or in spectacular festivity. Announcements are made in local media. Congratulations and gifts are offered. Everyone does their best to support and uphold marriage as a solid and happy state of being.

Yet marriage is a mixed blessing, psychologically speaking. With every available contrivance Civilization has tried to give each ego a stable foundation for a loving, enduring union. It has used force. It has cajoled. It has whispered sweet nothings. But desperate egos too easily become jealous or confrontational or possessive. These are the same feelings that young infants experienced with their mothers. The unhappy lessons learned about intimate relationships from that very first symbiotic attachment torn asunder are permanently etched in subconscious memories.

The Scream by Munch

9. Order From Chaos

For 150,000 years human beings lived gregariously without defined social rules or philosophy. They were aware of all living things, how those living things acted and reacted and changed over time. The patterns of the natural world were understood. Nothing in life was erratic or without rational cause. Everything was self-evident. People behaved in the same way everyday. Their motivations were pragmatic. They took care of themselves and each other. They nourished themselves from the environment. They took and used from the world around them only what was necessary. A little more than 10,000 years ago human psyches were exposed to the Modern S-I process, and everything changed. The human mind no longer perceived a rational world. People were completely unpredictable. The interaction of human beings with the physical world was not always understood or predictable. Life was filled with confusion, antagonism, and miscommunication.

Ego-centric individuals broke the social bonds that had kept humanity alive. Disagreements, threats, and physical violence became common. Physical and emotional abuse of children, spouses, and neighbors arose. People stole, murdered, and raped. Groups found reason to band and confront other groups. Wars, heretofore unknown, became alternatives to peaceful coexistence.

The world was chaos.

The social foundation that had supported homo sapiens for 150,000 years had collapsed. Small groups of prehistoric hunter-gatherers had faced life with strong personal bonds. Each individual had had respect for, intimacy with, and trust in every other member of the group. Those ties were not of family or friendship. They were much deeper, less emotional, and without verbal definition. After the Modern S-I process arrived human bonding crumbled. Mistrust, fear, and self-obsessed thinking strained every social contact. Intimacies struggled against barriers of dishonesty and secrecy. Close family and friends were never above suspicion. Aggression and disrespect hid feelings of insecurity.

This epoch in the story of our species was a transition period. Damaged psyches were looking for answers. They were trying to figure how to survive in this world. Where the world had once been crystal clear, things had become blurred and fuzzy. Understanding human actions was beyond perceiving repeated patterns. There could be no rational observation of actions motivated by desperate egos. Attempting to learn social behaviors was beyond trial and error methods. Developing minds could no longer trust any conclusions they postulated about anything. All was mayhem and disorder.

Human beings can survive as individuals, but survival is much easier and more efficient as a social group. The question for our species was how to sustain a viable society when individuals were now motivated by egocentrism. The question was how to unite selfish, argumentative, narrow-minded people. It remains a question.

Ten thousand years ago Civilization came to the rescue. Civilization was an unconscious development. It evolved on its own, growing in size and direction as required. Its methods included force and coercion, rules and regulation, and hierarchal structures. It appealed to ego and in turn was driven by ego.

To save humanity Civilization imposed an order on the chaos of the world. It charted a mathematical grid over the world. It outlined, mapped, and graphed human progress. It orchestrated social behavior and systematized social thought.

Exactly what changed with the advent of Civilization? We need merely look at the "before and after" differences in human society. Hunter-gatherers versus Civilized men.

There was a 99% flip in social behavior. There had been no rules or regulations, no rites, no taboos; no marriages. Civilization brought all of these things in spades. There had been social equality without nuance. Civilization brought individual authority, rank, and power structures.

There was also a 99% flip in the relationship of human beings to the natural world. The world itself did not suddenly crumble and fall into disarray 10,000 years ago. But the human species, as the sum of each and every individual human being, seemed to think so. Human beings were no longer an integral part of life and nature. They were outsiders and enemies. Civilization brought philosophy and religion. Civilization brought magic and supernatural.

Competition, hierarchies, philosophy, and supernatural have only existed since the beginnings of Civilization. They have only existed since the Modern S-I process required individual ego. A society made up of individuals with aggressive antagonism and self-centered motivations could not survive. Civilization imposed order.

It should be obvious that many aspects of Civilization were created to stabilize the social ravages of ego.

Competition exists only to show one better than another, a winner and a loser. When we realize that simple hunter-gatherers were not competitive in any way, that they survived cooperatively for 150,000 years, one questions the need for, or a rationale for, competition in human society. It is a vestment of Civilization. It exists to support ego.

Hierarchies, too, exist only to define some persons as better than others. Hierarchies establish image-boosting inequality without requiring actual competition for status. Hierarchies are not necessary in human societies. They are necessary in Civilized societies. They exist to support ego.

Whatever reasons Civilization has put forth to validate instituted competitions and hierarchies the underlying truth is that they only exist to support human egos.

Ten thousand years ago Civilization recognized each individual's need to give itself definition. It recognized the dissolution of social connections. It recognized the egocentric mind's need to establish a relationship with the natural world.

To quell every ego's fight for recognition it regulated every type of competition and established ranks of power, status, and wealth.

To define a human self-image it created philosophy and history.

To rebuild social bonds it imposed social order and the rules by which it would function.

To give ego its place beyond the limits of this world it founded religions. To help men overcome the perceived antagonism with the natural world it created Supernatural. To allow men to control nature it conjured magic.

Civilization was the means and method of creating order from chaos. Civilization did this by imposing its own abstract structure and architecture.

The strategy of Civilization is a group effort. Civilization is a social contract, an agreement by all to accept certain rules and behaviors as good and proper.

"Homo sapiens" translates as "wise man". But the words really only apply to Civilized men who coined the term. Simple hunter-gatherers such as our prehistoric ancestors were not wise. They were not self-aware. They did not give themselves or our species honorifics. They lived as a simple part of the natural world without ever recognizing that they were unique or separate, never needing to define a relationship between themselves and anything else; never needing to define themselves.

Civilization, needing to define structure and order for frail egos, has gone to great lengths to explain how human beings are unique and special. We are God's last and best creation. We are stewards of the earth and all therein. We are superior to other living things because we have language, because we make tools, because we think abstractly, because we are self-conscious, or because we compose and appreciate various art forms. We are the culmination of evolution. There is not a Civilized man on earth who does not have the bias that human beings are special and superior to other life forms. The world and all therein have become subjects of an anthropocentric universe.

Civilization as a contract is also an agreement to accept certain views of the physical world as correct.

No person can observe Planet Earth spinning on its axis and traveling in orbit around the sun. Yet Modern cultures consider any other explanation of the sun-planet relationship to be nonscientific. Any person who does not believe that the Earth spins and orbits the sun is considered uneducated and/or stupid. Say what you will about scientific proof, the fact is only by academic agreement. It is not evident to sensory perception. It is an imposed order established by Civilization. Homo sapiens thrived for 150,000 years without contemplating the relationships of sun and earth and moon.

The imposed structure of Civilization has become all-inclusive.

Civilization continues to examine and dissect the physical world with its various sciences of geology, biology, meteorology, and physics. We analyze, categorize, and alter the natural realm. But humanity remains without any intimate relationship to the world in which it lives. Civilization has fostered the idea that Mankind and Nature are antagonists at war with each other. Everything that man attempts must overcome or withstand natural forces. Natural resources are for the use of men. Men must shape the world for maximum human survival and comfort.

Civilization has placed humanity as the protagonist of history. Simple hunter-gatherer societies kept no oral histories. Our prehistoric ancestors had no need for history. But Modern psyches require individuals to define themselves, to place themselves in a continuum of time. Egos draw support from genealogies and lauded forebears. History ensures the bias that everything persons or peoples do is important. History is an ego-boost for every human, living or dead.

Civilization has adorned the landscape of our planet with global borders, longitude and latitude, and real estate offerings. Human intellectual abstractions have been superimposed upon grassy plains and river basins and mountain ranges. The soil beneath our feet is owned and taxed. The geological environment has been clothed in political, cultural, and financial finery. The natural world is first and foremost a realm of the human mind.

Civilization, in order to soothe every Modern psyche, has spun a magnificent web of mythological narrative. Seeking identity, abandoned Modern psyches have found themselves confronted by unanswerable questions of purpose and motivation. What am I? Why am I here? What is Life? What is my relationship to other people? What is my relationship to the world? It is a psychological chaos that requires order. Civilization has done its best to resolve the situation via intellectual abstraction. Individuals no longer need to float through life without answers. Philosophies have become guidelines for buoying and anchoring psyches. They give preassembled answers to the who, what, where, when, and why of Life. Religions, too, offer ready definitions for social context and relating to Nature. Religions offer the added finiteness of rules and rites which help to establish order. Unfortunately, Civilization has not been able to have humanity agree on an Ultimate Answer. Philosophies and religions have been fostered under various conditions and within many cultures so that they are not always in sync with everyone's ideas. Yet because they are intellectually abstract they need not adhere to fact. They are flexible and amenable, and are therefore effective frameworks within which to define individual personae.

Self-centered individuals do not thrive in social closeness. They do not lend themselves to cooperative effort.

They argue, lie, cheat, and condescend. People really cannot live together and work together under these circumstances. Even small groups of family and friends will fall apart. Ten thousand years ago Civilization gave order to the chaos of disintegrating societies. It imposed a structure of right and wrong on human behavior. It told everyone what was good and acceptable and what was not.

It was done out of necessity.

With the Modern S-I process there is a profound need for individuals to understand how to interact with other people. Everyone is ego-centric, but there is a recognized need to associate with others. Simply observing behaviors in others offers no clues for young minds. There are too many undecipherable motivations. Children must be taught. That is the role of Civilization.

Respect your elders.

Do not hit someone else.

Tell the truth.

None of the above are observable social behaviors in our societies. We have become prone to argument, insult, and badgering. Respect for anyone is minimal. Physical expressions of punishment or anger are commonplace. Truth is relative, and few feel any need to espouse it. We are selfish by our very psychological natures, so it is Civilization that must teach children to share and, "Do unto others as you would have them do unto you."

Laws against homicide and suicide must be taught. Good character must be taught, as it is not easily found to emulate. Generosity and selflessness must be defined by Civilization as they are not inherent qualities of Modern men. In spite of social and religious indoctrinations, self-centered behaviors still pervade. Cheating on exams and on income taxes, lying to close friends and under oath; taking more than an equal share and stealing from stores: all expose the need for Civilization's imposing of social order.

Civilization made social decisions easier by defining right and wrong. Young minds no longer needed to evaluate all human interactions to comprehend morality. One did not have to discover social truths by oneself. They were clearly defined and readily available. Rules and guidelines of ethics and morals established the standard. Etiquettes of speaking politely, greeting strangers, eating in social company, and standing in a crowd were given. Proper ways of debating an argument, of expressing grief, and of showing ardor were all predefined. Yet following these verbalized regulations seems to have been troublesome. Behaviors needed more and stricter definitions. There were social rules and political regulations and religious catechisms. Punishments were defined. Police forces, judicial courts, and penal institutions were established. Religions took punishment into the realms of afterlife and eternity. Right and wrong were elevated to philosophical absolutes, and every human being became a pawn in the "War between Good and Evil".

Good and Evil did not exist before 10,000 years ago. We need only look to our distant ancestors. Selfish behavior did not exist among simple hunter-gatherers. They had no need for rules of social correctness, no need for morals or ethics. As young infants they learned by observing those around them to live openly, peacefully, and respectfully.

Removing the trappings of Civilization we can see that all of this talk about Good versus Evil has really been about selfish desire versus consideration for others.

The social bonds of family and friends have been taught as obvious and strong. But no self-oriented infant feels these things. They are acquired as social education taught by Civilization. Sibling rivalry actually creates barriers between brothers and sisters close in age. But Civilization teaches that blood is thicker than water and that family sticks together. Fathers and mothers are to be respected whether they are caring parents or not.

Civilization's rules have become so accepted that they supersede rational evaluation. Bonds of family and friendship are supported whether or not the persons of family and friends are of good character or not. Criminals, murderers, and rapists are supported by friends and family even after all of their behaviors have become public.

Likewise, Civilization has trained us to accept abstract social parameters rather easily. A master of ceremonies can arbitrarily divide an audience into Groups A, B, and C. He can ask for cheers and applause from each group. With this simple request he can generate a spirit of rivalry and, equally, a spirit of camaraderie among complete strangers of varied backgrounds, intellects, and beliefs.

It is worth noting that in attempting to teach proper behavior Civilization finds it necessary to begin with the self. How should we love our neighbor? "Love thy neighbor as thyself." How should we treat others? "Do unto others as you would have them do unto you." The rationale behind these admonitions for social equality is still a focus on oneself. They are addressed to individuals whose thinking will always be egocentric.

For the past 10,000 years Civilization has been taught to children and adults. It is the solution to the perceived chaos in the Modern world. It is the survival strategy that has enabled homo sapiens to continue to thrive. Unfortunately, there is an inherent weakness in this necessary strategy. It depends on verbal communication to define rules and rank and morality. Verbal communication can only be acquired after one year of an infant's life experience. There will forever be a gap between the knowledge an infant gains from observation by its five senses during its pre-verbal months and the socially indoctrinated knowledge it is taught by Civilization through the abstract symbolism of language.

**Do
as
I
say
not
as
I
do
!**

10. Words and Language

If Civilization was the means and method of creating order from chaos, then words were the mechanism which enabled Civilization.

Homo sapiens have always had language. They are social beings. Our prehistoric ancestors chatted and related the day's events. But human language used to be different.

Look at any page of any dictionary. You will find that 99% of the words therein only exist to support Modern psyches and/or Civilization. Eighty percent of those words have no connection to any physical reality but are founded on the abstract symbolism of other words.

The languages of our prehistoric ancestors were devoid of all the words that have been sown by the Seed of Civilization.

There were no words of competition and comparative evaluation. There were no winners and losers. There were no social elites, no down-trodden masses; no conquerors or vanquished.

There were no words of introspection.

There were no words of imaginary things, no Supernatural; no unknowns to ponder.

There were no words of violence, aggression, revenge, or hatred. The emotions of Modern Civilized man are different. We know envy, condescension, anger, and pride. We scheme; we insult, we cajole, we betray. We swear undying loyalty and eternal hatred.

To simple hunter-gatherers, to all of our prehistoric ancestors, this would have been incomprehensible.

An understanding of words is not innate. Words must be taught and acquired.

Human beings learn by two methods. We learn by observation which includes seeing, hearing, touching, smelling, and tasting, and we learn by verbal instruction which includes listening and reading. We are born with our senses, but we begin without a comprehension of language. With constant urging by family and friends this begins at six to nine months and continues throughout a lifetime. Infants begin to imitate speech at about one year.

Before the Seed of Civilization, before the ego needed recognition, human language was simple. Words had a one-to-one relation with the natural world. Our Paleolithic ancestors named objects, actions, and phenomena. Plants and animals had names. Actions such as walking, throwing, and running had names. Wind, thunder, and sickness had names. Children did not learn about these things from words. They experienced some natural thing and were taught a word to associate with the object or event.

This was sufficient for our prehistoric ancestors who did not need rules and did not rely on words to understand life. But for those who cannot perceive an ordered world learning by words is essential. The complexities of Civilization cannot be learned by observation. If we cannot learn by seeing, we must be taught by language.

The education of every infant, of every new homo sapiens, of every new member of human society has undergone a shift from 99% experiential learning through the five senses to 99% acquired verbal teaching by words. The import of this fact is almost beyond our Modern ability to comprehend. It explains why the same world of air and water and living things and the same physical experience of being born and maturing and eventually dying was so different for prehistoric people. Their world was never dressed in the Emperor's New Clothes of Civilization.

Civilization requires words to function. Without words there are no rules. Without words there is no religious mythology. Without words there is no political structure. All of these things are founded in concepts that exist only through the words that created them. These concepts cannot be learned by observation of the natural world, but, incredibly, these ideas can be imposed on the natural world. With verbally biased minds we can find justification for our concepts in Nature. Civilization and humanity triumph because they have the words to say so.

Civilization used abstract symbolic language to accomplish three things:
to teach order and social behavior;
to assuage and bolster weak, incomplete, unconfident egos;
to alter the techniques by which our minds think, the methods by which we evaluate and make judgements.

Civilization's words have imposed pattern and purpose on the natural world. Words have codified social structure and law. Words have tutored personal ethics and moral conscience.

Let us consider how Civilization has taught us to recognize some patterns of the physical world:

Time places events in sequence without beginning or end. Time itself is structured in increments of seconds, minutes, hours, days, years and centuries.

Three-dimensions give spatial relation and volume to geometric shapes. All physical things have three dimensions. One- and two-dimensional objects are theoretical and exist only in human imaginations.

Creation stories, whether scientific or mythological, define a beginning to our physical world. When human egos found it necessary to characterize themselves, knowing where and when people originated was important.

Maps are abstract symbols of the soil and firmness we walk upon. They show political and cultural boundaries. They indicate relative locations of cities, rivers, mountains, and deserts. They teach us about an environment well beyond what we will ever experience.

Mathematics is a quantitative analysis of the world around us. Numbers are its unique symbolic language. Representation of physical truths is extrapolated into infinities of imaginary symbolic truths that can rarely be explained in a tangible, sensory way.

Physics translates obvious observations into Laws, e.g. an object at rest will remain at rest until acted upon by an outside force. Once Laws are stated as verbal abstractions they can be manipulated to man's imagination. We analyze the world from within our minds rather than observing what is in the natural world.

Biology has placed all living things into well-ordered hierarchies. It has given us Plant and Animal Kingdoms. It has made sure that human beings are ensconced in the upper echelon of all living things.

All of these ideas and intellectual concepts have been imprinted and overlaid on the physical world in which we find ourselves. They exist to create patterns which Modern human beings can see and define around themselves. By words such as these Civilization has attempted to satisfy the psychological needs of Modern men. Please note that early human beings had no need of such things. Nor do other living things have need of such things.

Similarly, Civilization has taught us the guidelines for a functional human society:

Right and wrong give people binary choice. The verbal labels free the mind from needing to evaluate social interactions. One simply applies society's rules or prepares for the consequences of not agreeing.

Truth is an absolute which need not be questioned. For psyches adrift in a chaotic world it is the ultimate assurance.

Respect is instruction to self-centered individuals who must be taught how to get along with other humans.

Loyalty is a social adhesive. Egotistic people will reflexively act only for themselves. They must be infused with concepts of family, friendship, camaraderie, and patriotism.

Promises and vows are a method of having individuals act in a consistent way. Surprisingly, they rely on an individual's self-image as an honest person to function.

Almost all of the social education a person receives during his lifetime is by abstract concepts founded in verbal symbolism.

It was by words that Civilization was able to coddle and calm frail egos. It encouraged them. It desensitized their emotional over-reactions. It supported their needs for attention and praise. Civilization persuaded selfish, ruthless, antagonistic egos to live and work together. This was done mostly by regulating competition and instituting social and political hierarchies. When those were not sufficient Civilization brought forth special concepts:

Altruism and philanthropy are care for others instilled in ego-centric individuals. They are compassion for others but still hold the benefit of honoring oneself.

Reward is simply recognition. It can be for many things, but it is one of the necessities of an insecure ego. "You've earned a gold star!" "You are special!" "You will find reward in the Afterlife!"

Well-liked, good-looking, and *fun* are a few of the thousands of clever adjectives created to compliment self-centered individuals for nothing special. None of these qualities would ensure survival in the natural world.

As words and language became the modus operandi of Civilization, the human mind altered its functional operating system.

Children learned about life from words. They learned of things they would never experience and of animals that they would never see. They learned to translate experience into numbers, religious predestination, or evidence of scientific law. Adults ignored sensory information in favor of mental meanderings. The world became anthropocentric. The world was no longer perceived by human beings. Human beings conceived the world around them.

Words became more real than life experience. The abstract symbolism of language superseded biological and evolutional imperatives of survival.

Consider the following words which have been built by Civilization completely from verbal abstraction:

Economics is a study of human relations based on financial structures. Money, wealth, business, and economic value are all symbolic realities. They exist only as human society gives them acceptance. Somewhat ironically, the physical reality of banks and stock markets was created from symbolic abstraction of financial development without any base in physical reality. Money from money.

Career is the concept of living one's life with a focus on certain achievement goals related to occupation or avocation. Planning and making decisions based on purpose and success is completely based on cerebral ideas.

Prehistory is a recent cerebral development. Civilization gave people history when egos needed to characterize themselves. Civilization gave men concepts of the past, a time continuum, heritage, and a portrait of our species and its motivations. Eventually it added a concept of evolution and a distant past. It then needed "prehistory", a word to define what came before all that we knew. Prehistory only exists as a spin-off of history which exists as the self-portrait of Civilized man.

The minds of Modern men function very differently from the brains of other species. Indeed, the minds of Modern men function very differently from the minds of early homo sapiens.

The sensory data of life experience is no longer important. What is important is how that information is processed. When a Civilized human being looks at a tree he or she no longer sees the physical reality of that tree. One does not notice its health or its age or if it is bearing seeds. Civilized men see a large member of the Plant kingdom. They recognize that it can be useful as shade, as a source of food, or as a source of wood for fuel, construction, or carving. The information that the Modern human mind takes in is verbally biased.

The development of every human infant, its intellect and its personality, depends on verbal indoctrination. It is an unfortunate necessity. Verbal teaching and learning especially at an early age create psychological constancy and consistency when the young child cannot find these in experiential reality.

Law and Order, Crime and Punishment, Political Science

Our hunter-gatherer forebears lived together without rules or taboos. They lived cooperatively with respect and consideration for all.

How, then, did humanity get from having no social regulation to having law libraries, police departments, and constitutional governments with executive, legislative, and judicial branches? How did we arrive at admonitions to "Obey the Law" and "Live an Honest Life"?

Over time Civilization has had to imagine an increasing number of verbal concepts to educate and order individuals' behaviors. It has had to fight egos at every point. By creating ever more abstract interpretations of acceptable behavior, egos have been tricked into agreeing to society's "One for All, and All for One!"

Notice the progression of abstract concepts:
Our ancestors gently corrected their children or members of the group if they strayed from acceptable behavior. They would quietly redirect children or stop them from misbehaving, which they did very rarely. Adults were laughed at if they made a social faux pas. In return the transgressor would laugh and say it had all been a joke... how could anyone think a person would do such a silly thing?

After the Seed of Civilization Modern children trying to emulate adults were constantly admonished. "No! No! No!"

In spite of its continuing popularity this reprimanding is rather ineffective. It does not teach what is acceptable behavior. It merely teaches what is not acceptable behavior.
The concept of Bad came later. It is a nonspecific for inappropriate behavior. It was accusatory. The original intent was for the accuser to feel superior by scolding another.
When Good for society and Good for a self-centered individual became confused, Good and Bad soon needed to be translated to more abstract concepts of Right and Wrong. Right and Wrong were more theoretical and less capricious. Even today appropriate behavior is not taught as Good for society. There will always be an incomprehensible struggle between pleasing oneself and acting for the well-being of others. An ego-centric individual cannot understand the rationale for supporting a group unless it gains for itself. So Right and Wrong enter a philosophical world.
When Right and Wrong had to be taught to generation after generation they became formalized via verbal rules. It was too difficult for Modern humans to continually interpret intellectually abstract concepts of Right and Wrong. Rules could be remembered and related easily in words. One did not need to understand a philosophical argument about supporting communal Good. One simply followed rules.
Society found that rules quite often needed clarification and caveats. They became codified as Law. Rules and laws were not always accepted by all members of society. So society found that laws with appropriate punishments might deter inappropriate behavior. It was the thinking of people who find solutions by dominating others. Right became Law and Order. Wrong became Crime and Punishment.

Of necessity Civilization has translated the experience of living life in a social environment into living life with strict adherence to a world created by words and verbal abstraction.

Design by Erte

11. Competition

Competition would seem to be the most natural thing in the world. Species compete for evolutionary survival. Predators compete for food. Flowering plants compete for sunlight. As Civilized human beings we find competition in all the world around us. But competition is not the way of all living things. Herd animals support each other by living and traveling side-by-side. They share food and water. Antarctic penguins huddle en masse to protect themselves through brutal, sub-zero winters as they care for the eggs of the next generation. Bees, ants, tuna, herring, and flamingos live socially in large groups. Symbiotic species live off one another to the benefit of each.

The Polar Eskimos and the Kalahari Ju/wasi did not have competition. They assiduously avoided it. Our simple hunter-gatherer ancestors lived the same, cooperatively and with perfect social equanimity for 150,000 years.

We justify competition as building physical and mental skills, but our early ancestors simply practiced a skill until it was sufficiently acquired. They did not need an opponent to beat.

For Modern human beings competition is as instinctive as trying to hold your breath longer than the guy next to you. Every aspect of life is competition. Life is a rat race, a challenge, an endurance match, and an uphill battle.

Most obviously, we compete by way of sports and athletic feats. Running faster than someone else, throwing a javelin further, and even punching someone until they can no longer stand may be considered as having real life applications. But hitting a ball with a stick to earn runs or putting it into a cup on the green or hitting it back and forth over a net are not life skills. Shooting a ball through a hoop, smacking a black rubber puck on ice, and rolling a ball into ten pins are not talents for survival. Yet in today's world one can earn a good living by doing exactly these things. There are professional sports of every kind. Civilization has created thousands of activities that test every imaginable physical prowess: the three legged race, the sack race, catching greased pigs, spitting watermelon pits, tiddlywinks, and mumbly peg. Even we are amused by the inanity of it all.

Every physical feat is performed against an opponent or opponents or a clock or an existing record. It is always competition. Victory is sweet, and defeat is sour. We count wins and try to forget losses. Our egos feed but wish for more. So Civilization tallies not only wins but has every sport keep continuing accounts of an infinity of game statistics to compare all player's abilities. We eke out as much glory as possible for as many as possible.

Not everyone can compete physically and win. Not even with an infinity of crazy games and stunts. So people have looked to compete at other things and in other ways to get attention and to feel superior. Supported by Civilization they have found plenty.

Admittedly, in comparison to other species homo sapiens are not especially endowed with physical talents. We have survived on cunning and brain power. Civilization took those virtues and made it possible for egos to excel at mental competitions instead of athletic contests. Competing with our brains requires no physical skills whatsoever.

There are hundreds of popular games that require agile minds. Chess and go are the recognized acme of intellectual games. Tic-tac-toe, played all around the world, may be the nadir. But they are all competitions with winners and losers.

Civilization has established myriad ways for individuals to show off intellectually. Game shows, IQ tests, Trivial Pursuit, riddles, and every kind of puzzle solving are mental challenges that can flaunt and glorify ego.

Academic knowledge, good memory, or an extensive vocabulary bring recognition to individuals. Reasoning powers of clear logic and rational deduction are highly praised. An articulate debater or an eloquent orator wins popular acclaim. All of these qualities are most frequently showcased in a competitive setting. In school we compete for grades. At work we compete for advancement and salary. In politics we compete for votes and power. In public we compete for adoration. All for attention and adulation; all for ego.

Not everyone is satisfied with simply gaining recognition as having better physical or mental abilities. Not everyone is capable of gaining recognition with their physical or mental abilities. These individuals still have egos to sustain. If there is no way to support those egos there will be discontent and resentment. Society will be confronted with an unhappy, disruptive section of its population. These people may be healthy and well-fed, but their egos are unsatisfied.

To meet the demand for competitive success Civilization found other ways for people to compete. There is no aspect of our lives that is without competition. We compete for friends and lovers. We compete for money and status. We compete for respectability and the moral high ground. We seek and accept praise for beauty, fashion, humor, pets, cars, houses, and cooking. We compare ourselves with those around us in regard to every little thing. There is no end to our ego's covetousness.

Aggressive competition was founded in the psychological insecurity and sibling rivalry of the Modern S-I process. It readily explains the collapse of egalitarian society and of social cooperation in prehistory. Competition could easily have been the end of our entire species. Competition could have been the last man standing.

The psychological profiles of Modern humans make them fervently pursue competition. Excelling at any competition gives their egos what egos crave. Egos created competition to get notice and praise from others.

The goal of competition is not self-satisfaction. Ego demands prestige. Competition is self exaltation at the expense of others. Competition by its very definition is antagonistic and hostile.

What Civilization has done is give ego its due while at the same time curbing and redirecting competition to make it socially acceptable. Civilization took the aggression and the desire for acclaim that pervaded ego-driven humans and domesticated it. It would have been too much to ask to eliminate the deep-rooted psychological motivation. Civilization could not eliminate ego. But tempering it with rules and limits allowed people to live together. Not an easy task.

How did Civilization subdue competition? It used the power and persuasiveness of words.

Ego needs constant reassurance. A competitive victory may be obvious, but it is momentary. Ego needs to show the world how significant this win was. Ego needs to broadcast and record and perpetuate each victory. If not, an individual will need to compete again and again. How many times must victory be repeated to keep an ego satisfactorily nourished?

Words allow one victory to be remembered and memorialized for generations. This is only possible through language. Being able to verbally register an event, to make it a part of history, has allowed Civilization to quell overly aggressive psyches.

Civilization also chose to spread the wealth of competitive achievement to a broader field of participants. Why should only one runner be lauded for a successful race? Simply by using words Civilization created "win, place, show" and "gold, silver, bronze". In one competition there are enough accolades for several egos. Why should only competitors be allowed to emotionally profit from winning? Civilization encouraged spectators and fans to feel psychological elation merely by supporting the victors.

Words functioned so well that competitions could often be avoided simply by talking. Simple hunter-gatherers had all been "good" hunters. They were never compared to their friends and neighbors. "Good" was sufficient, and nothing more was needed. But Modern men could not accept simply being equal to others. They needed to be honored and esteemed. Civilization created a whole new genre of words: comparatives and superlatives. Individuals could now brag that they were "better". If too many made the claim of being better, someone could outmaneuver them and be "the best". Such words need not have any evidence for the assertion. Certainly fast, faster, and fastest could be tested. But verbal concepts made way for attributes that would forever be moot: cute, cuter, and cutest; lively, livelier, and liveliest; funny, funnier, and funniest. All of these are qualities that an ego will accept praise for. All are founded solely in verbal abstraction.

Words were also the mechanism by which Civilization calmed competitive frenzy and in turn assuaged frenzied egos. Civilization declared that if competitions were to be a part of human endeavor then they would be given rules and protocols. Competition no longer needed to be open-ended. Competitions became sports and contests and pageants. Time limits, strict measuring, and regulating officials were established for sports. Contests and pageants were given venues, strict criteria, and judges.

Without words and verbal thinking it is impossible to define parameters and specifications for sports and games. Today there are thick volumes of rules and regulations for every professional sport. There are books filled with analysis and strategy. There are training manuals, histories, and statistical records.

Abstract symbolic thinking has also made it possible to imagine complex options and objectives in a game or sport. The Olympic triple-jump and pentathlon; football's touchdown, field goal, and extra-points; and numerous variations of billiards demonstrate the creativity of verbal thinking pertaining to competition.

Competitive egos being what they are, even words have become a game medium with such things as crossword puzzles, spelling bees, Scrabble, and the Daily Jumble.

Ego thrives on competition, and for ten millennia competition has driven Civilization.

War

War is the ultimate competition.

War is easy. Ever since the psychological shift that set individuals against each other, aggressive antagonism has attached itself to the human race. We may have strict rules and enforcement against antisocial behaviors, but war has not succumbed to the control of words. In fact, words have often been used to instigate and inflame wars.

War has never been domesticated; it has never been Civilized. Hostility is too deep-rooted in human psyches. War stimulates egos to reflexive actions, to kill or be killed. Ego senses sibling rivalry, the primal psychological fear. Once the vestments of Civilization are doffed and the ego is bared there is actually great psychological satisfaction in killing and hurting and dominating others. All of this is against the biological and evolutionary imperatives of survival of the species and the individual.

Try as she might, Civilization cannot forge psychic restraints from iron. It is difficult to convince egos that anything is more important than they themselves are. Very difficult.

Explaining the origins of war has been a dubious academic pursuit. There is really no credible evidence from any time before Civilization's city-states raised armies and went into battle. That fact has not stopped scholars from putting forth learned conjecture. Common explanations are that humans have always fought amongst themselves, that war came with the advent of agriculture, or that war is a natural part of biological and evolutionary behavior when overcrowding occurs.

Inherent aggression within our species seems reasonable enough when faced with the whole of human history and current events. There has never been a time in history when there was not armed conflict somewhere in the world. It is a perpetual pastime of dictators, colonists, and zealous demagogues. Disagreement is best settled by annihilation of the weaker party. Scholars point out that many species are inherently aggressive and kill. But there is slim truth to that. Predator species are seemingly violent in that they hunt and kill for food. They do not kill for any other reason. Humans killing humans has no such rationale. Predators often live and hunt in packs that have a hierarchal social structure. But predators do not kill each other. They may fight for rank within the power structure, but the defeated are not slain. They will leave the pack or remain subservient. Humans fight on a much larger scale to more decisive ends. Some mammalian males will fight each other only during mating periods. They do not fight otherwise. They are not inherently aggressive. Seasonally elevated sex hormones control the antagonistic behavior. Human males only occasionally fight for women in barrooms and in movies.

The excuse that violence is inherent in homo sapiens falls flat when confronted with facts regarding simple hunter-gatherer societies. All who have come into contact with and/or studied these peoples have been astonished at the lack of competitive, aggressive, and disruptive behaviors. They remark over and over how these "harmless" and "gentle" people do not confront one another or fight. If a member of the clan cannot resolve a difference of opinion he or she simply goes to live with another group. If intruders from the outside Civilized world encroach, nomadic hunter-gatherers will move along to find another land that will support them. They are skilled hunters who do not lack confidence or courage in any way, but they do not become combative in situations Civilized humans would find intolerable.

Simple hunter-gatherer societies are not aberrations of human lifestyle. They were the norm for 150,000 years. Violence is not inherent in our species, only in our Modern cultures.

Many scholars of human prehistory logically place warlike behavior at the advent of agriculture. They make the claim that permanent settlements and bountiful food supplies led to an accumulation of wealth and spurred human jealousy and greed. There would seem to be at least several holes in this theory. With a plentitude of food and material goods why would someone want more, indeed more than they could logically use? Of what practical purpose was looting gold and silver? If neighbors or outsiders wanted to steal the benefits of agriculture, was killing the best way to achieve this? War would seem to be much more work with a greater risk of failure than actual farming. There is the claim that groups wanted more land for farming and went to battle to gain it. Why would a group want more farmland? Had the group grown beyond its means? How and why would that happen? Being covetous of farmland was little reason to attack and actually destroy the farmland in the process of besieging a walled city-state. None of these arguments make sense in the light of human personality before ten thousand years ago. There was no precedence for such behavior. Why would a people change their character so dramatically? Why become avaricious at all?

Some scholars see war as a factor in the natural selection process. Overpopulation in a species cannot be supported with a limited supply of natural resources. There is the possibility that the entire biological classification may go extinct. Because humans have no natural enemies, the argument goes, they increase beyond an acceptable limit. They are sturdy and exploit every possible resource. With no other evolutionary method capable of remedying the situation, human beings are forced to decimate themselves. In spite of grave misunderstandings regarding natural selection and the natural biological responses to overpopulation, i.e. decreasing fertility, disease, and/or malnutrition, this theoretical proposal seems to fail in the light of the ever-burgeoning number of humans inhabiting our planet. War has done nothing to limit our species. Humans have not controlled the population of their species by any means available to them.

Whereas academic theories seem to fade after thoughtful consideration, ego is a perfect raison d'être for war. Ego supports every reason for challenging others, for using force, for risking life and limb; for wanting what belongs to someone else. Ego is all about needing attention and respect. Ego is all about superiority and lording it over others. Ego is all about wealth and possessions. Ego is all about control: controlling one's destiny, controlling the actions of others, and controlling reality. Ego thrives on anger and bullying. Ego knows it is right and others are wrong.

Unwittingly, Civilization became ego's comrade. Civilization brought power far beyond any individual's abilities. Civilization taught strength in numbers and hierarchal allegiance. Men and nations go to war as directed and inspired by their leaders. There is seldom a need to convince subordinates of finite purpose or goal. Men fight for God, for Country, and for Freedom. These ideas are verbal abstractions. They are concepts taught by Civilization.

Words, Civilization's abstract symbolism, have transmuted biological survival from imperative to whim.

12. Hierarchies

A hierarchy of any kind serves what purpose? A Civilized person will say that a hierarchy gives order and structure to society. Hierarchies allow societies to function easier and more efficiently. They are necessary. They give definition.
But it is not true. It was certainly not true for our Paleolithic ancestors or for their forefathers. The Polar Eskimos and the Kalahari Ju/wasi did not have hierarchies or social strata of any kind. Their lives, their opinions, and their motivations were egalitarian. Everyone had equal status. There was no alpha-male. No one's opinion held more weight than another's. We often characterize them as strong individualists, holding their own counsel. That is from our own biased view. In truth, their motivations were never self-centered. They were confident, but their decisions were made in consideration of the whole group. If they hunted separately it was simply because only one man was necessary and because it was more efficient. They labored in groups if that was more efficient at the moment. Everyone carefully avoided any situation that would give him or her prominence or higher regard. No one desired to be better than any of the others. Social harmony and equality were the desired status quo.
Hierarchies are anathema to egalitarian societies. They foster and maintain inequality. Someone is better than another. Some together are better than other groups. To what end do hierarchies exist, especially if they were unnecessary (and carefully avoided) for 150,000 years?
Quite simply, hierarchies support egos. That is their origin and nurture. The Modern Separation-Individuation process is an integral step in the development of every Civilized human child's psychological personality. It is characterized by building both an ego and an individual's identity in competition with others. Long before he or she can walk an infant learns that it must struggle for attention and support. It is helpless without them. The infant senses that it is in a struggle for life itself. The young child is desperate and fraught with trauma.
Competitions are the most conspicuous display of ego's craving. Competition requires effort and energy on the part of individuals. Hierarchies do not. They boost many egos without any struggle at all.

Hierarchies in a society do exactly the opposite of maintaining social equality. They attempt to coddle and placate desperate egos by making them feel special and unique. Hierarchies categorize individuals, give them titles, and segregate them from the general populace. Everyone may live side-by-side, but Civilization has made sure that each ego knows it is better in some way than those people around it. Hierarchical valuations may give prestige, but it is in name only. There is no assurance of material benefit. Superiority is often unearned and without merit. Those ranked as low class can seldom shake off the label.

The extent and variety of social classifications show how much value Civilization has put on hierarchies. Power, wealth, and fame bracket everyone with status or a lack thereof.

Political power is one of the most beguiling of hierarchies. It allows egos to command, to laud it over underlings, and to accept ingratiating behaviors from subordinates. Even those caught in the middle ranks of power strata can dominate the lowest. Underlings often get the satisfaction of token rewards and recognition from those above them. They also boost their egos with the knowledge that their superiors are really not so superior, that superiors seldom know what is going on under their noses, and that superiors are not the ones doing the work that keeps things going. The most powerful individuals place their importance above day-to-day activities. They contemplate their places in history. They sense Destiny and the Hand of God.

Political power is not about government. It is about authoritarian structure. It is about everyone having a ranked position and fitting into a rigid sequence from highest to lowest. It is about hierarchies that allow some people to direct and control parts of other people's lives. Every Civilized institution is set up in this way. Governments and military forces are the most obvious. Modern governments establish police departments and judicial courts to ensure adherence to the law. Every company and enterprise has leaders and management. Banks, hospitals, and philanthropic organizations do also. Churches and universities have governing bodies and subordinate ranked positions.

Wealth has long been used by Civilization to place individuals and families into a class structured hierarchy. Real estate, entrepreneurial net worth, monetary reserves, and ostentatious displays of affluence are approvingly recognized by society. Philanthropy, which simply means that one has enough money to give away freely, is likewise lauded by Civilization. Ego has been the driving force behind accumulating wealth. Initially, hoarding material goods gave reassurance to insecure psyches. The idea was perpetuated that possessions were an indication of a person's success and importance in life. The person with the most money wins. Everyone can be socially evaluated by their net worth. For many Civilized men and women money has been the primary, and often single, motivation in life. It seems to satisfy their egos on many levels.

Social classes based on power and monetary worth are not enough to sustain a population fraught with voracious egos. Not everyone can have too much money. Those who do not have so much money still need to feel better than their neighbors. Civilization has contrived dozens of other ways for individuals to feel superior.

Fame is the most prominent ego booster. It is not tangible on any level. It requires neither power nor financial base. It is elusive. Yet it is a most compelling status that is open to entertainers, athletes, politicians, authors, and even academicians and scientists. Most recently it has become available to anyone who can take a selfie and post it on the internet. There is no clear criterion for what makes an individual famous, but fame lifts individuals to elite caliber and bursts egos with self-adulation.

Subtle categories of social hierarchies filter our lives daily. There is status for hundreds of Modern human qualities. Physical beauty, likability, attraction to the opposite sex, sense of humor, and the ability to have a conversation are all things we judge in others. In turn, we are evaluated with similar criteria by others. We heighten our personalities and physical attributes with fashion: clothing, shoes, make-up, hair color and style, sunglasses, and handbags. Anything that will attract attention. It is a field day for egos. If one hesitates to consider these as hierarchal, think of the words we associate with fashion: haute couture, elegant, dapper, classic, stylish, au courant, modest, out of fashion, passé, dowdy, shabby, frumpy, etc.

Civilization's hierarchies are often rigorous. The position of husband and father as head of household has often been a license to control and abuse other members of the family. It is a position freely given and clearly defined by

Civilization. It requires no justification or qualifications, but it is supported by law courts and religious institutions unilaterally. Religion has created a unique opportunity for people to rank each other on the bias of relating to the Supernatural. Not only may individuals feel holier than thou, but they can be closer to God and speak more intimately with God. Egos love this type of self aggrandizing for it is impossible to refute.

In the more recent Modern societies academic hierarchies are a fact of life from an early age. In schools we are evaluated and graded continuously from the very first day. We are compared to our classmates and to students across the state, across the country, and around the world. Schools are ranked, and there is much prestige in attending elite universities. Degrees are awarded to show achievement through well-defined levels of accredited institutions of learning. There are strict protocols for academic faculties. Careers and advancement at the work place are strongly linked to the educational credentials framed and hung on office walls.

Nowhere is the strict stratification by Civilization more evident than in the world of sports. Athletic competition has global organizations to regulate play and players. There are professional, semi-pro and amateur levels. Standings of teams and players is adjusted daily and covers grade school, collegiate, professional, and international levels. Within the organizational system of many sports, especially the martial arts, one rises through the ranks as one's skill increases. At any moment an athlete will know exactly where he or she fits into the sport's hierarchy.

Without Civilization none of these hierarchical distinctions would be significant. They serve no purpose other than bolstering egos. In a more pragmatic world where it would be understood that food is man's primary need, hunters and farmers would be at the top of human societies not kings or bishops or CEO's.

While establishing social hierarchies has served Civilization well, the process has been arbitrary. There is no good reason that human societies have become patriarchal. Some may argue that biology places males above females, but Polar Eskimos, Kalahari Ju/wasi, and our prehistoric ancestors disprove the claim. Men and women in simple hunter-gatherer groups relied on each other and never considered either more important than the other. They were equal partners. Patriarchy or matriarchy was a binary choice, a coin toss, made 10,000 years ago and perpetuated until today. Male domination has been pervasive and does everything in its power to maintain its claim of superiority over women.

Hierarchies in our Modern societies have come to serve individual's psyches beyond the stabilizing of greedy egos. They are a bulwark for defining object constancy. They are acquired by verbal learning, and once learned they give everyone a seemingly unchanging view of how individuals function in society. Hierarchies fix an order to human interactions: who has authority; who must be respected and shown deference; who can be looked down upon or ignored. Establishing these guidelines frees ego-based individuals from having to think through each encounter with another person. One simply follows the rules of social etiquette. It is a simple choice: is this person of higher rank or not? Circumstance may temporarily change who is in charge, e.g. a tyrannical dictator if very sick will defer to his doctor. But Civilization has given clear structure. Everyone can understand their place. There is a consistency and permanence to the behavior of those around us. This psychological stability explains why lower classes are not in constant rebellion and why wives will stay with abusive husbands. Constancy is more important than freedom.

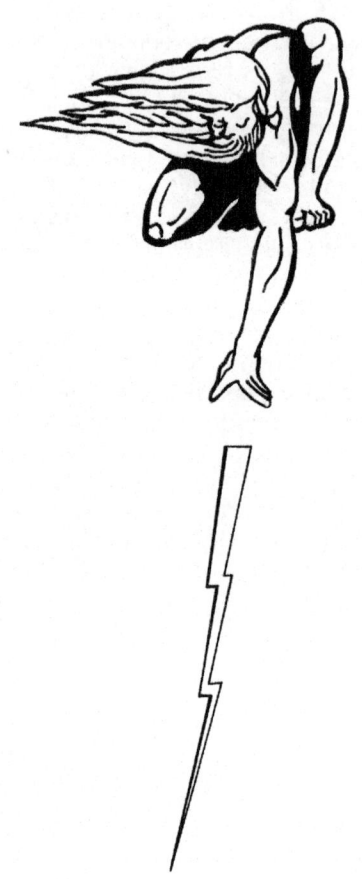

13. Supernatural

When the new psychology of human beings met agriculture 10,000 years ago Civilization's creativity was given another impossible task. Efforts at growing crops and domesticating animals placed men at odds with the natural order. That conflict needed to be resolved in men's favor.

The beginnings of agriculture are a mystery. It seems doubtful that people with Archaic SI psychologies would have even attempted agriculture. It is more likely that they would have continued to hunt and gather from the bounty that surrounded them. But humans have always been observant and creative. Permanent settlements at native grain fields (such as those of the Natufian culture in the Levant circa 14,000 - 11,000 years ago) may have initiated attempts at agriculture.

Humans who endure a Modern SI development feel that they must fend for themselves. There is a desperation within them. Ten thousand years ago they would not have been happy to rely on natural resources if they could create a better situation. They were avaricious. They were insecure. They were arrogant. Agriculture and animal domestication would have appealed to ego-driven people.

They committed themselves to their own ingenuity. They took from nature, then improved on nature, demanding more and more from the species they domesticated. They altered landscapes to establish fields and farms. They built fences to keep domestic animals in, and they built fences to keep wild animals out. When there was not enough natural rainfall they irrigated fields. When their animals could not graze properly they grew crops to feed the livestock.

Consciously or not, agriculture was a choice, a commitment to live in one place and cultivate sustenance rather than seek it out. At some point the growing dependence on agriculture became a real problem. Agriculture was a difficult proposition. For nomadic hunter-gatherers survival had always been within an individual's capable abilities. For the sedentary farmer crop cultivation was not always within his management. Agriculture was dependent on weather, soil conditions, and freedom from natural infestations of plant diseases and insects. No matter how well cared for, how intelligently observed, or how much work and energy was put in, the success of harvests was not

100% controllable or predictable. The eventual realization of this was humbling and frightening.
As people put their efforts and faith in agriculture they lost their intimate relationship with the world around them. They no longer studied their environment with the keen senses hunters and gatherers used to ensure survival. They no longer felt the need to limit birth rates and control population growth.
At some point agricultural achievement failed. Blight, locusts, or lack of rainfall severely limited or wiped out the expected harvests. People did not know what to do. Crops might return next season, but that was a long way off, and there was no guarantee of renewed success. People could no longer easily pick up and move on as their nomadic ancestors had. Ego-centric individuals and societies had nowhere to turn to for help and no one to blame but themselves.
Civilization came to the rescue. It conjured magic and the idea of altering physical reality by curious acts and murmured words. Then it named God as Supernatural, more powerful than and able to control Nature. Because by themselves men could not control nature. Because ego-centric human beings were at the whim and mercy of a seemingly capricious world. They needed help.

The Polar Eskimos and the Kalahari Ju/wasi did not have religious beliefs or symbolic rites or magical incantations. They had no amulets or ritual dances for bountiful hunting. There is no reason to believe that our prehistoric ancestors had religious beliefs or social rites. There was no belief in a Supernatural that could control the Natural world. There were no mystical rites of passage into adulthood. There was no symbolic ritual to accompany an individual's birth or death. It should be noted that burial does not imply rite or ritual. Burial was a pragmatic solution to a dead body. Artifacts found with a body do not in any way imply a belief in a hereafter; they simply belonged to the deceased and were of no use to anyone else.
Simple hunter-gatherers did not wish to alter the course of natural events. It would never have occurred to them. It was not a part of their psychological make-up. They grew up in a finite world. They observed and adapted. They learned how something new fit into the scheme of things.

Magic was created by Modern psyches who could not accept unpleasant happenings. Magic was initiated by the coincidence of random events. Without the foundation of a strong object consistency, these human minds never fully grasped physical reality or common sense. Associating good fortune with talismans, finding bad omens in unusual behaviors, and re-enacting gestures or sounds to recreate happy circumstance seemed logical enough. They were the same psyches that insisted something might still work even after a hundred failures, that lead could be turned to gold, and that one could speak to the dearly departed. When physical and mental skills could not overcome adversity, people sought trickery. Magic was an arcane, mysterious talent with endless potential. Only ego-centric humans could have given themselves such assistance in dealing with a hostile world. Only ego-centric humans would have felt they faced a hostile world.

Magic was a necessary precursor to Supernatural. Magic opened minds to the possibility of things lurking out of sight, to the manipulation of experiential reality, and to the possibility of powerful forces yet to be unleashed.

The realization of Supernatural was a stroke of genius. Civilization calmed countless ego fears at once. Supernatural was above and beyond Natural. Supernatural was completely new, beyond the five senses, imperceivable. The word alone was sufficient for one to imagine its power and immensity. Supernatural was infinite, omniscient, and omnipresent. It appealed to egos to have an ally with limitless might. Supernatural could alter and control Nature. All humans had to do was appeal to the Supernatural, call upon the gods, pledge troth and fealty. Their prayers would be answered.

The beauty of Civilization's concept of deity is that, while it can never be proven, it can also never be disproven. If wishes and desires are answered, no more proof of a divine power is necessary. If prayers are left unanswered then humans may have to make a little bit more effort, implore more earnestly, offer gifts and sacrifices. It is something that aligns perfectly with ego-centric thinking.

Religion was an institutionalizing of man's relationship to the Supernatural. Religion systematized the new holy realms of Supernatural. Hierarchal structure was put into place so that everyone understood their relative position in relation to the Almighty. It laid down the ground rules and rationally dissected every nuance of things that could not be known. Because in the same way that Modern psyches needed verbal instruction and rules for social behaviors,

Modern psyches needed to be guided in their relationship with the Supernatural.

God must be taught, and that is what religion did. Clearly there were no patterns for the human brain to observe. People had to be told who Deity was and how it functioned. People were taught how to have God intercede on their behalf.

With the guidance of religion the realm of Supernatural changed the identity of human beings. Religion offered answers to unfulfilled psyches who wanted desperately to define themselves. It placed humanity beyond and more important than the physical world in which men now lived. It was a tremendous ego boost. Life could now be a spiritual journey or a war between Good and Evil or the ultimate test by God for the salvation of a sacred soul.

The omniscience, omnipresence, and omnipotence of deity exist only as words. These are abstract concepts built from abstract concepts, none of which can ever be derived from life experience. They are only words, verbal symbolic thinking. For Modern Civilized men, however, these words are sufficient to instill fear, awe, and obedience.

Magic, Supernatural, and religion are not inherent human understandings. We must be taught to imagine them. We must be taught with words that step beyond the reality of physical experience. That is something our prehistoric ancestors did not do. When people lived intimately with the natural world they had no need of magic or Supernatural.

Supernatural is not a sixth sense.
Supernatural is not of this world.
Neither are fantasy, superstition, horror, or melodrama.

These things are not innate or intrinsic or instinctive. These things are not since the beginning of time. They were born 10,000 years ago when there was a psychological shift in the homo sapiens species.

These things only came into being after the Seed of Civilization was sown. They were birthed by words and grew as verbal thinking grew. They are not of the physical world. They are not of the natural world. They are meta-physical. They are Super-natural.

Woman by Picasso

14. Conclusion

Human beings have not always been who they are today. For thousands of generations Stone Age homo sapiens were nomadic and semi-nomadic peoples. They hunted for meat and gathered vegetable foods when available. They lived in small groups of 25 to 35 individuals. They shared meat among all. They did not argue or complain. They gave no thought to themselves. About 10,000 years ago there was an obvious 99% shift in the life style and the behavior of the species. Our species stepped outside of the natural world. They began living in permanent dwellings and cities. They domesticated plants and animals. They started fighting amongst themselves and killing each other. They became arrogant and selfish. The Seed of Civilization was planted, and something unique in all life experience was created.

Homo sapiens had always been gifted with highly functioning brains. The Seed of Civilization shifted those minds into overdrive. For better or worse our Modern Civilized minds function differently from any other living species, contemporary or extinct. That is not the result of a genetic coding unique to our species. Modern homo sapiens do not function by verbal abstraction because of peculiar DNA. Homo sapiens do not carry a gene for marriage vows and philosophy. Team sports and gold medals are not entwined on double helix molecules. Modern human beings are not unique in nature because of their biology. They are unique because of their psychology.

The Seed of Civilization is psychological.

All that Civilized men have created has been driven by psychological need.

We are not who we are because it is human nature to be so.

The key to this understanding is the realization that homo sapiens have changed. We began as one human nature then became another. We have not always been Civilized.

There is ample archeological evidence. There is ample anthropological evidence.

There was not a slow, gradual evolution to Civilization. The evidence of Civilization is pretty easy to find. Modern men have left metal artifacts and imposing architecture. Clay pottery, woven fabrics, walled cities, and stamped coins attest to human societies well ensconced in Modern sedentary life. These things can be found all around the world. They cannot be found dating back more than 10,000 years when the Seed of Civilization shot up and sprang to life. Within 2,000 to 3,000 years it was a vital, thriving organism.

There are also clues to mankind's earlier life. Admittedly, the evidence has been adulterated and, at this point in time, is almost non-existent. We can obviously find evidence of Civilization, but Civilization, agriculture, and global transportation have left almost no trace of the hunter-gatherer societies that reveal the character of our prehistoric ancestors. We have recorded accounts of Polar Eskimos and Kalahari Ju/wasi and perhaps one or two more societies. Even these accounts must be read with the understanding that they are subtly biased by Civilized thinking.

The recorded accounts of simple hunter-gatherers untouched by Modern Civilization reveals these people and their societies to have been very different from every other known human culture. Very different. They had no chiefs, headmen, or priests. They were non-competitive in every aspect of their lives. Their societies were egalitarian and cooperative. They had no religion, ritual, or rites. They did not have marriage practices. We have always assumed human societies to have leaders, religion, rites and hierarchies. We have assumed humans to be inherently competitive.

We can be quite certain that our prehistoric ancestors survived for 150,000 years as nomadic hunter-gatherers. There is archeological evidence to support this and none to refute it. It makes sense on every level of analysis.

There is no evidence of warfare or religion before 10,000 years ago.

Prehistoric cave art dating from between 35,000 years ago and 12,000 years ago gives strong support for human thinking that was not anthropocentric. Art since 10,000 years ago has been 99% about humans.

There is evidence in academic research that has been overlooked. It has been thought that human emotions today are the same as for all men who have ever lived. It was assumed that all human beings have had the same psychological and biological motivations. It may have been a logical assumption. Unfortunately, it was incorrect. There have been obvious anomalies observed in hunter-gatherer societies by sociologists and anthropologists. Small bands of people lived peacefully without aggression or leadership or taboos. They were considered to be simply curiosities of human experience. In truth, they are the remnants of what all human societies once were.

It is important to realize that Civilized society is not required by nature. Prehistoric human beings and human societies did not require religion, social rules, or government. Civilized societies DO require these things because the psychological character of people changed. Human beings are now ego-centric, self-centered. This is not meant as necessarily being selfish and only doing things for themselves.

But it is a psychological reality that today's individuals feel that the only true, real thing they can be sure of in life is themselves. Everything else is questionable. That is the psychological reality, and that is why Civilization established religion, governments, and social rules to help people through life.

We are not the same human character as our prehistoric ancestors. With the awareness of this dichotomy in the personality of homo sapiens there is now a new baseline for academic studies. The insights presented in this book change the way we must perceive every academic pursuit.

Philosophy must have a new focus. It is no longer a question of defining reality and life. It is rather a question of defining Civilized humanity's perception of reality and life.

Biology must no longer be used as the excuse for human aggression. Human behavior can no longer to be extrapolated by comparison to animal behaviors of other species.

Psychology must accept that the Separation-Individuation process which characterizes the natural psychological development of every human child from birth is only true for Modern Civilized infants. Psychology must look at human emotions and define them in terms of prehistory. Psychology must also accept that human beings are not inherently aggressive and competitive. These behaviors are acquired, not genetically programmed.

Linguistics must define the differences in human speech before and after the Seed of Civilization. That kernel created a need for a greater degree of verbal abstraction. Language before the Seed of Civilization was simpler, in one-

to-one correspondence with the physical world. Linguistics can now show how language became the root of Civilization, creating social inequality, fantasy, and an anthropocentric universe. Because, in truth, these things exist only through language.
History must accept the ramifications of what it means to be "Civilized".
The study of prehistory must be rewritten. It is no longer a shadowy past to be filled with imaginative conjecture. We can accurately define the lifestyle of our species for 150,000 years. We can explain the prehistoric cave art of France and Spain without hypothesizing motives of magic or Supernatural.
Sociology and ethnology must rephrase the questions they use to characterize and define human societies and human behaviors.
Anthropology must accept that it now has the proper tools with which to define prehistoric human societies. It must look at human experience on this planet as being influenced by agriculture, birthrates, and human psychological development.
Art history will accede that prehistoric cave art was a unique achievement. It was created by inspiration from the parietal wall surfaces and had no emotional or intellectual intent. The art shows creative and stylistic genius, but it had no other motive than graphic aesthetics.
Political science now has a finite origin and motive... the ego of Civilized man.
Ethics and morality now have a finite origin and motive... the ego of Civilized man.
Religion and religious beliefs now have a finite origin and motive... the ego of Civilized man.

The insights in this book have lessons for every human being living today.
Knowing that violence is not a natural part of our species we are offered new options for resolving disagreement. Indeed it should be clear that there is less need for argument and confrontation. Human beings lived cooperatively for 150,000 years. We can no longer use the excuse that human beings are inherently prone to violence, murder, and rape. Recognizing ego as the source of our malcontent places the onus of acceptable behavior on ourselves.

Knowing that competition is not a natural part of our species we are free to choose how we participate in sports and games. There is no longer valid support for winning at all costs. There is no need to abuse opponents or cheat or use performance enhancing drugs. We can concentrate on the physical and mental skills demanded by our contests. We can congratulate opponents and appreciate every players' athletic prowess and strategic adroitness without dwelling on victory and loss. Competition is no longer necessary at the work place or at social gatherings or in the home. We can acknowledge that living life need not be in comparison to others.

Knowing that hierarchies are not a natural part of our species we can look upon each other as equals. Façades and affected airs can be dropped. Status in fashion and glamor can become a pleasant pastime and not a contest. Cars can simply function as transportation, and handbags will carry personal items. Attempts to belittle or control others can be ignored with the understanding that a weak ego is simply trying to assert itself.

Knowing that magic and Supernatural are not a natural part of our human species we can consider more appropriate decision making. We can study religious philosophy from a new perspective. We can look at the rationale for a theocentric world view.

Knowing that we have been subconsciously at the desire and command of our frail and desperate egos actually frees every person who has endured the Modern Separation-Individuation process to overcome early traumas. We are free to self examine our behaviors and motivations in a new light. We are free to understand those around us and to explain all human actions throughout history. We are free to interpret the Seed of Civilization and how it grew.

We now know that the motivations for human beings are not the biological and evolutional motivations of every other living creature. For 150,000 years homo sapiens were indeed simply motivated by such. But there was an unforeseeable mishap when biological survival became too easy. With a plentitude of nutritional resources humans began to over-populate. Now Modern Civilized man is motivated by psychological deprivation. It is doubtful that this will ever change. Ego, once released, cannot be put back in the comfortable box from which it came.

Humanity is not doomed to be forever at the mercy of its psychological impairment. There is a unique loophole in the cloth of our psychological shroud. Verbal abstraction, words, the tools by which Civilization has kept us from self-annihilation, can incline the human mind to almost anything. Words have created many unnatural realities for people. People have believed and continue to believe the most fantastic things simply because words can shape them.

Words have a strange power. Once something has been defined and given a verbal symbol human beings can work with it or against it quite easily.

Alcoholics Anonymous has stated that the first step to curing addiction is to verbalize the condition. "Hello, my name is Bill, and I am an alcoholic." Consulting psychiatrists ask patients to talk about their problems and to put things into words. Without such preliminaries a patient will never deal with their phobias, compulsions, or neuroses.

Our Civilized brains function with a verbal operating system. That operating system has seemingly limitless capabilities and talents. Words alone will not bring a person to choose a better lifestyle or etiquette. But they offer the option to improve if one cares to. We no longer have to be prisoners to psychological traumas from infancy.

We live in a different world from our ancestors. It is a world of our own making.

From a humble and desperate beginning the Seed of Civilization has brought forth incredible and miraculous things. Romantic love, heartwarming drama, and spiritual inspiration exist only because of Civilization. Masterpieces of art, monuments of architecture, and marvels of intricate machinery are the progeny of Civilization. A manned space station, microchips, heart transplants, global finance, bullet trains, and lie detectors are achievements of Civilization.

So are high heels, nouvelle cuisine, and tourism.

Nuclear weapons, the electric chair, slavery, holy wars, and genocide are consequences of Modern Civilized society. Our planet supports at least 700% more humans than it should. All of nature suffers under manmade climate change and pollution. Entire species have been rendered extinct by mankind.

Created from a rogue Seed, Civilization was born of necessity. It has functioned surprisingly well, but it has been a mixed blessing. Because it is egocentric it has operated with a narrow focus. Because it is without natural constraint it has advanced unchecked.

In spite of every natural, biological, and evolutional law to the contrary the homo sapiens species has eked out survival for a tumultuous 10,000 years.

Bibliography

Freuchen, Peter
Book of the Eskimos
copyright © 1961 by Peter Freuchen Estate
World Publishing Company, Cleveland

Hodder, Ian
The Leopard's Tale, Revealing the Mysteries of Çatalhöyük
copyright © 2006 by Thames & Hudson, Ltd.
Thames & Hudson, Ltd., London
ISBN 0-500-05141-0

Lee, Richard B. and DeVore, Irven, editors
Kalahari Hunter-Gatherers: Studies of the !Kung San and Their Neighbors
copyright © 1976 by the President and Fellows of Harvard College
Harvard University Press, Cambridge Massachusetts
ISBN 0-674-49985-9

Mahler, Margaret S.
and Fred Pine, and Anni Bergman
The Psychological Birth of the Human Infant
copyright © 1975 by Margaret Mahler
Basic Books
ISBN 0-465-06659-3

Marshall, Lorna J.
The !Kung of Nyae Nyae
copyright © 1976 by Lorna Marshall
Harvard University Press, Cambridge, Massachusetts
ISBN 0-674-50569-7

Nyae Nyae !Kung Beliefs and Rites
copyright © 1999 by the President and Fellows of Harvard College
Harvard University, Cambridge Massachusetts
ISBN 0-87365-908-2

Mead, Margaret, ed.
Cooperation and Competition Among Primitive Peoples
copyright © 1937 by McGraw-Hill Book Company, Inc.
McGraw-Hill Book Company, Inc., New York

Thomas, Elizabeth Marshall
The Harmless People
copyright © 1958 by Elizabeth Marshall Thomas
Random House, Inc., New York

The Old Way
copyright © 2006 by Elizabeth Marshall Thomas
Picador, New York
ISBN-13: 978-0-312-42728-3
ISBN-10: 0-312-42728-X

Printed in Great Britain
by Amazon